Music and Imagination

THE CHARLES ELIOT NORTON LECTURES

1951–1952

MUSIC AND IMAGINATION

By Aaron Copland

HARVARD *University Press* • *Cambridge*
Massachusetts • *London* • *England*

Library of Congress Catalog Card Number 52–9385

ISBN 0–674–58915–7

Printed in the United States of America

Preface

THE PAGES THAT FOLLOW comprise the Charles Eliot Norton Lectures delivered at Harvard University during the academic year 1951–1952. They appear here in substantially the same form in which they were read to the students and general public at Cambridge. The six talks were not intended to be closely reasoned arguments on a single subject, but rather a free improvisation on the general theme of the role imagination plays in the art of music. The first half of the book treats of the musical mind at work in its different capacities as listener, interpreter, or creator. The second half discusses more specifically recent manifestations of the imaginative mind in the music of Europe and the Americas.

The lectures were followed in each instance by short concerts made possible by the generosity of the Elizabeth Sprague Coolidge Foundation in the Library of Congress and the Norton Professorship Committee of Harvard University. It is a pleasure to be able to record here my thanks for their coöperation. I am deeply appreciative also to the many fine artists who took part in these concerts. Their names will be found listed at the back of this book.

Grateful acknowledgment is due the Norton Professorship Committee for their cordial reception during my stay in Cambridge, and especially to its literary and musical representatives, Professors Archibald MacLeish and A. Tillman Merritt, friends of long standing, who were ready at all times with helpful guidance.

A word of thanks is also due to Miss Eleanor Bates of the editorial staff of the Harvard University Press for her keen and cogent criticism during the preparation of the manuscript for publication.

A. C.

Cambridge, Massachusetts
May 1952

CONTENTS

ix

Music and Imagination

Introduction

IT PLEASES ME to think that Charles Eliot Norton might have approved the appointment, in 1951 for the first time, of a native-born composer to the Poetry Chair established in his memory a quarter of a century ago. The thought that it was I myself who had been entrusted with this high responsibility made me sensibly less happy. To address the student body at Harvard in the tradition of the learned scholars and poets and composers who had preceded me as incumbents of the Norton Chair was not an easy task. Fortunately, this same tradition sanctioned a free interpretation of my title as poetry professor, so that I was able to discuss the one thing I profess to know something about: the art of music.

Perhaps I had better begin by frankly admitting that when I was a younger man I used to harbor a secret feeling of commiseration for poets. To my mind poets were men who were trying to make music with nothing but words at their command. I suppose there exist at all times some few men who have that much magic in them, but words at best will always seem to a composer a poor substitute for tones — if you want to make music, that is. Later on, after I had had some slight reading acquaintance with the poetry of Hart Crane and Gerard Manley Hopkins, I came gradually to see that music and poetry were perhaps closer kin than I had at first realized. I came gradually to see that beyond the music of both arts there is an essence that joins them — an area where the meanings behind the notes and the meaning beyond the words spring from some common source.

If that is true, if poets and composers take flight from a similar impulse, then perhaps I am more of a poetry professor than I had

1

thought. The music of poetry must forever escape me, no doubt, but the poetry of music is always with me. It signifies that largest part of our emotive life — the part that *sings*. Purposeful singing is what concerns most composers most of their lives. Purposeful singing to me signifies that a composer has come into possession of musical materials of related orders of experience; given these, the composer's problem then is to shape them coherently so that they are intelligible in themselves, and hence, communicable to an audience. In music the process does not stop there. The musical work must be reinterpreted, or better still, re-created in the mind of the performer or group of performers. Finally the message, so to speak, reaches the ear of the listener, who must then relive in his own mind the completed revelation of the composer's thought.

This very familiar recital of the musical experience suddenly takes on, as I tell it, the aspect of a very hazardous undertaking. It is hazardous because at so many points it can break down; at no point can you seize the musical experience and hold it. Unlike that moment in a film when a still shot suddenly immobilizes a complete scene, a single musical moment immobilized makes audible only one chord, which in itself is comparatively meaningless. This never-ending flow of music *forces* us to use our imaginations, for music is in a continual state of becoming. Wystan Auden, who knows a great deal about verse and song, recently made this distinction between the two. "A verbal art like poetry," he wrote, "is reflective; it stops to think. Music is immediate; it goes on to become." This elusive quality of music, its imagined existence in time, is made the climax of Jean Paul Sartre's treatise on *L'Imaginaire*. Sartre, in a well-known passage on Beethoven's Seventh Symphony, very nearly succeeds in convincing us that the Seventh isn't really there at all. It's not on the page, for no music can be said to exist on the silent page, and it's not in any one performance, for they are all different and not one can be said to be *the* definitive version. The Seventh, Sartre says, can only be said to live, if it does live, in the unreal

2

world of our imagination. Whatever one may think of Sartre's theory, it dramatizes one of the basic facts in music — a fact to which we shall return more than once in these pages.

What I have set down here I have learned from my own experience in the writing of music and in considering the music of other composers. These reflections, I should add, are not meant to be a contribution to knowledge: the typical artist cannot be said to function on the level of knowledge. (I use the word in its usual meaning of learning and scholarship.) I can only hope to speak to you on the plane of intuitional perception — the plane of immediate or sensitive knowledge — perceptual knowledge, if you like. This is an important distinction — at least for me it is — because it makes clear that those of us who are doers rather than knowers expect others to deduce knowledge from the testimony we bear. This is not to say, as sometimes is said, that a composer describing a musical state of affairs is doing nothing more than describing his own musical tastes. A composer's apperceptions need not necessarily be so circumscribed as that. A well-known conductor once confided to me that he invariably learned something from watching a composer conduct his own composition, despite possible technical shortcomings in conducting, for something essential about the nature of the piece was likely to be revealed. I should like to think that an analogous situation obtains when a composer articulates as best he can the ideas and conceptions that underlie his writing or his listening to music. If my conductor friend was right, the composer ought to bring an awareness and insight to the understanding of music that critics, musicologists, and music historians might put to good use, thereby enriching the whole field of musical investigations.

Thus it is primarily as a composer — a musically observant composer, posing temporarily in the guise of a professor of poetry — that I have chosen to consider the general topic of the relation of the imaginative mind to different aspects of the art of music.

3

Part One

MUSIC AND THE
IMAGINATIVE MIND

CHAPTER ONE

The Gifted Listener

THE MORE I LIVE the life of music the more I am convinced that it is the freely imaginative mind that is at the core of all vital music making and music listening. When Coleridge put down his famous phrase, "the sense of musical delight, with the power of producing it, is a gift of the imagination," he was referring, of course, to the musical delights of poetry. But it seems to me even more true when applied to the musical delights of music. An imaginative mind is essential to the creation of art in any medium, but it is even more essential in music precisely because music provides the broadest possible vista for the imagination since it is the freest, the most abstract, the least fettered of all the arts: no story content, no pictorial representation, no regularity of meter, no strict limitation of frame need hamper the intuitive functioning of the imaginative mind. In saying this I am not forgetting that music has its disciplines: its strict forms and regular rhythms, and even in some cases its programmatic content. Music as mathematics, music as architecture or as image, music in any static, seizable form has always held fascination for the lay mind. But as a musician, what fascinates me is the thought that by its very nature music invites imaginative treatment, and that the facts of music, so called, are only meaningful insofar as the imagination is given free play. It is for this reason that I wish to consider especially those facets of music that are open to the creative influences of the imagination.

7

Imagination in the listener — in the gifted listener — is what concerns us here. It is so often assumed that music's principal stumbling block is the backward listener that it might be instructive to contemplate for a change the qualities of the sensitive listener.

Listening is a talent, and like any other talent or gift, we possess it in varying degrees. I have found among music-lovers a marked tendency to underestimate and mistrust this talent, rather than to overestimate it. The reason for these feelings of inferiority are difficult to determine. Since there is no reliable way of measuring the gift for listening, there is no reliable way of reassuring those who misjudge themselves. I should say that there are two principal requisites for talented listening: first, the ability to open oneself up to musical experience; and secondly, the ability to evaluate critically that experience. Neither of these is possible without a certain native gift. Listening implies an inborn talent of some degree, which, again like any other talent, can be trained and developed. This talent has a certain "purity" about it. We exercise it, so to speak, for ourselves alone; there is nothing to be gained from it in a material sense. Listening is its own reward; there are no prizes to be won, no contests of creative listening. But I hold that person fortunate who has the gift, for there are few pleasures in art greater than the secure sense that one can recognize beauty when one comes upon it.

When I speak of the gifted listener I am thinking of the nonmusician primarily, of the listener who intends to retain his amateur status. It is the thought of just such a listener that excites the composer in me. I know, or I think I know, how the professional musician will react to music. But with the amateur it is different; one never can be sure how he will react. Nothing really tells him what he should be hearing, no treatise or chart or guide can ever sufficiently pull together the various strands of a complex piece of music — only the inrushing floodlight of one's own imagination can do that. Recognizing the beautiful in an abstract art like music partakes

8

somewhat of a minor miracle; each time it happens I remain slightly incredulous.

The situation of the professional musician as listener, especially of the composer, is rather different. He is an initiate. Like the minister before the altar his contact with the Source gives him an inner understanding of music's mysteries, and a greater familiarity in their presence. He possesses a dual awareness: on the one hand of the inscrutable mystery that gives certain common tones meaning; on the other of the human travail that enters into every creation. It is an awareness that no layman can hope to share. There is a nicety of balance in the musician's awareness that escapes the musical amateur. The amateur may be either too reverent or too carried away; too much in love with the separate section or too limited in his enthusiasm for a single school or composer. Mere professionalism, however, is not at all a guarantee of intelligent listening. Executant ability, even of the highest order, is no guarantee of instinct in judgment. The sensitive amateur, just because he lacks the prejudices and preconceptions of the professional musician, is sometimes a surer guide to the true quality of a piece of music. The ideal listener, it seems to me, would combine the preparation of the trained professional with the innocence of the intuitive amateur.

All musicians, creators and performers alike, think of the gifted listener as a key figure in the musical universe. I should like, if I can, to track down the source of this gift, and to consider the type of musical experience which is most characteristically his.

The ideal listener, above all else, possesses the ability to lend himself to the power of music. The power of music to move us is something quite special as an artistic phenomenon. My intention is not to delve into its basis in physics — my scientific equipment is much too rudimentary — but rather to concentrate on its emotional overtones. Contrary to what you might expect, I do not hold that music has the power to move us beyond any of the other arts. To me the theater has this power in a more naked form, a power that is almost too great. The sense of being overwhelmed by the events that occur on a stage sometimes brings with it a kind of resentment at the ease with which the dramatist plays upon my emotions. I feel like a keyboard on which he can improvise any tune he pleases. There is no resisting, my emotions have the upper hand, but my mind keeps protesting: by what right does the playwright do this to me? Not infrequently I have been moved to tears in the theater; never at music. Why never at music? Because there is something about music that keeps its distance even at the moment that it engulfs us. It is at the same time outside and away from us and inside and part of us. In one sense it dwarfs us, and in another we master it. We are led on and on, and yet in some strange way we never lose control. It is the very nature of music to give us the distillation of sentiments, the essence of experience transfused and heightened and expressed in such fashion that we may contemplate it at the same instant that we are swayed by it. When the gifted listener lends himself to the power of music, he gets both the "event" and the idealization of the "event"; he is inside the "event," so to speak, even though the music keeps what Edward Bullough rightly terms its "psychical distance."

What another layman, Paul Claudel, wrote about the listener seems to me to have been well observed. "We absorb him into the concert," Claudel says. "He is no longer anything but expectation and attention . . ." I like that, because expectancy denotes the ability to lend oneself, to lend oneself eagerly to the thing heard, while attention bespeaks an interest in the thing said, a preoccupation with an understanding of what is being heard. I've watched the absorbed listener in the concert hall numerous times, half absorbed myself in trying to fathom the exact nature of his response. This is an especially fascinating pastime when the listener happens to be listening to one's own music. At such times I am concerned not so much with whatever pleasure the music may be giving, but rather with the question whether I am being understood.

Parenthetically, I should like to call attention to a curious bit of artist psychology: the thought that my music might, or might not give pleasure to a considerable number of music-lovers has never particularly stirred me. At times I have been vigorously hissed, at other times as vigorously applauded; in both circumstances I remain comparatively unmoved. Why should that be? Probably because I feel in some way detached from the end result. The writing of it gives me pleasure, especially when it seems to come off; but once out of my hands the work takes on a life of its own. In a similar way I can imagine a father who takes no personal credit for the beauty of a much admired daughter. This must mean that the artist (or father) considers himself an unwitting instrument whose satisfaction is not to produce beauty, but simply to produce.

But to return to my absorbed listener. The interesting question, then, is not whether he is deriving pleasure, but rather, whether he is understanding the import of the music. And if he has understood, then I must ask: *what* has he understood?

As you see, I am warily approaching one of the thorniest problems in aesthetics, namely, the meaning of music. The semanticist who investigates the meaning of words, or even the meaning of meaning, has an easy time of it by comparison with the hardy soul who ventures forth in quest of music's meaning. A composer might easily side-step the issue; aesthetics is not his province. His gift is one of expression, not of theoretic speculation. Still the problem persists, and the musical practitioner ought to have something to say that would be of interest to the mind that philosophizes about art.

I have seldom read a statement about the meaning of music, if seriously expressed, that did not seem to me to have some basis in truth. From this I conclude that music is many-sided and can be approached from many different angles. Basically, however, two

11

opposing theories have been advanced by the aestheticians as to music's significance. One is that the meaning of music, if there is any meaning, must be sought in the music itself, for music has no extramusical connotation; and the other is that music is a language without a dictionary whose symbols are interpreted by the listener according to some unwritten esperanto of the emotions. The more I consider these two theories the more it seems to me that they are bound together more closely than is generally supposed, and for this reason: music as a symbolic language of psychological and expressive value can only be made evident through "music itself," while music which is said to mean only itself sets up patterns of sound which inevitably suggest some kind of connotation in the mind of the listener, even if only to connote the joy of music making for its own sake. Whichever it may be, pure or impure, an object or a language, I cannot get it out of my head that all composers derive their impulse from a similar drive. I cannot be persuaded that Bach, when he penned the *Orgelbüchlein,* thought he was creating an object of "just notes," or that Tchaikovsky in composing *Swan Lake* was wallowing in nothing but uncontrolled emotion. Notes can be manipulated as if they were objects, certainly — they can be made to do exercises, like a dancer. But it is only when these exerciselike patterns of sound take on meaning that they become music. There is historical justification for the weighted emphasis sometimes on one side, sometimes on the other, of this controversy. During periods when music became too cool and detached, too scholastically conventionalized, composers were enjoined to remember its origin as a language of the emotions, and when, during the last century, it became overly symptomatic of the inner *Sturm und Drang* of personalized emotion, composers were cautioned not to forget that music is a pure art of a self-contained beauty. This perennial dichotomy was neatly summarized by Eduard Hanslick, standard bearer for the "pure music" defenders of the nineteenth century, when he wrote that "an inward singing, and not an inward feeling, prompts a gifted person to compose a musical piece." But my point is that this dichotomous situation has no reality to a functioning composer. Singing *is* feeling to a composer, and the more intensely felt the singing, the purer the expression.

The precise meaning of music is a question that should never have been asked, and in any event will never elicit a precise answer. It is the literary mind that is disturbed by this imprecision. No true music-lover is troubled by the symbolic character of musical speech; on the contrary, it is this very imprecision that intrigues and activates the imagination. Whatever the semanticists of music may uncover, composers will blithely continue to articulate "subtle complexes of feeling that language cannot even name, let alone set forth." This last phrase I came upon in Susanne Langer's cogent chapter, "On Significance in Music." Reviewing the various theories of musical significance from Plato to Schopenhauer and from Roger Fry to recent psychoanalytical speculation, Mrs. Langer concludes: "Music is our myth of the inner life — a young, vital, and meaningful myth, of recent inspiration and still in its 'vegetative' growth." Musical myths — even more than folk myths — are subject to highly personalized interpretation, and there is no known method of guaranteeing that my interpretation will be a truer one than yours. I can only recommend reliance on one's own instinctive comprehension of the unverbalized symbolism of musical sounds.

All this is of minor concern to the gifted listener — primarily intent, as he should be, on the enjoyment of music. Without theories and without preconceived notions of what music ought to be, he lends himself as a sentient human being to the power of music. What often surprises me is the basically primitive nature of this relationship. From self-observation and from observing audience reaction I would be inclined to say that we all listen on an elementary plane of musical consciousness. I was startled to find this curious phrase in Santayana concerning music: "the most abstract of arts," he remarks, "serves the dumbest emotions." Yes, I like

13

this idea that we respond to music from a primal and almost brutish level — dumbly, as it were, for on that level we are firmly grounded. On that level, whatever the music may be, we experience basic reactions such as tension and release, density and transparency, a smooth or angry surface, the music's swellings and subsidings, its pushing forward or hanging back, its length, its speed, its thunders and whisperings — and a thousand other psychologically based reflections of our physical life of movement and gesture, and our inner, subconscious mental life. That is fundamentally the way we all hear music — gifted and ungifted alike — and all the analytical, historical, textual material on or about the music heard, interesting though it may be, cannot — and I venture to say should not — alter that fundamental relationship.

I stress this point, not so much because the layman is likely to forget it, but because the professional musician tends to lose sight of it. This does not signify, by any means, that I do not believe in the possibility of the refinement of musical taste. Quite the contrary. I am convinced that the higher forms of music imply a listener whose musical taste has been cultivated either through listening or through training or both. On a more modest level refinement in musical taste begins with the ability to distinguish subtle nuances of feeling. Anyone can tell the difference between a sad piece and a joyous one. The talented listener recognizes not merely the joyous quality of the piece, but also the specific shade of joyousness — whether it be troubled joy, delicate joy, carefree joy, hysterical joy, and so forth. I add "and so forth" advisedly, for it covers an infinitude of shadings that cannot be named, as I have named these few, because of music's incommensurability with language.

An important requirement for subtle listening is a mature understanding of the natural differences of musical expression to be anticipated in music of different epochs. An awareness of musical history should prepare the talented listener to distinguish stylistic differences, for example, in the expression of joyousness. Ecstatic joy as you find it in the music of Scriabin ought not to be sought for in the operas of Gluck, or even of Mozart. A sense of being "at home" in the world of the late fifteen hundreds makes one aware of what not to seek in the music of that period; and in like fashion, being "at home" in the musical idioms of the late baroque period will immediately suggest parallelisms with certain aspects of contemporary music. To approach all music in the vain hope that it will soothe one in the lush harmonies of the late nineteenth century is a common error of many present-day music-lovers.

One other gift is needed, this one perhaps the most difficult and at the same time the most essential: the gift of being able to see all around the structural framework of an extended piece of music. Next to fathoming the meanings of music, I find this point the most obscure in our understanding of the auditory faculty. Exactly in what manner we sort out and add up and realize in our own minds the impressions that can only be gained singly in the separate moments of the music's flowing past us is surely one of the rarer manifestations of consciousness. Here if anywhere the imagination must take fire. Sometimes it seems to me that I do not at all comprehend how other people put together a piece in their mind's ear. It is a difficult feat in any of the arts, especially those that exist in point of time, such as the drama or fiction. But there the chronology of events usually guides the spectator or reader. The structural organization of the dance is somewhat analogous to that of music, but here too, despite the fluidity of movement each separate moment presents a picture, not unlike that of the painter's canvas. But in music where there is no chronology of events, no momentary picture, nothing to "hang on to," as it were, it is the imagination and the imagination alone that has the power of balancing the combined impressions made by themes, rhythms, tone colors, harmonies, textures, dynamics, developments, contrasts.

I don't mean to make this more mysterious than it is. To draw a graph of a particular musical structure is generally possible, and may be of some help to the cultivated listener; but we do not usually wish to listen to music with diagrams in our laps. And if we did, I question the wisdom of such an idea, for too great concentration on the purely formal outlines of a piece of music might detract from free association with other elements in the piece.

No, however one turns the problem, we come back always to the curious gift that permits us to sum up the complex impressions of a piece of absolute music so that the incidents of the harmonic and melodic and textural flow of the work as it streams past us result finally in a unified and total image of the work's essence. Our success in this venture depends first on the clarity of the composer's conception, and second, on a delicate balance of heart and brain that makes it possible for us to be moved at the same instant that we retain the sensation of our emotional response, using it for balanced judgment later in other and different moments of response. Here, most of all, the listener must fall back upon his own gift; here, especially, analysis and experience and imagination must combine to give us the assurance that we have made our own the composer's complex of ideas.

Now, perhaps, is the moment to return to one of my principal queries: *what* has the listener understood? If anything was understood, then it must have been whatever it was the composer tried to communicate. Were you absorbed? Was your attention held? That, then, was it; for what you heard were patterns of sounds that represent the central core of the composer's being — or that aspect of it reflected in the particular work in question. One part of everything he is and knows is implicit in each composer's single work, and it is that central fact of his being that he hopes he has communicated.

It occurs to me to wonder: are you a better person for having heard a great work of art? Are you morally a better person, I mean? In the largest sense, I suppose you are, but in the more immediate sense, I doubt it. I doubt it because I have never seen it demonstrated. What happens is that a masterwork awakens in us reactions of a spiritual order that are already in us, only waiting to be aroused. When Beethoven's music exhorts us to "be noble," "be compassionate," "be strong," he awakens moral ideas that are already within us. His music cannot persuade: it makes evident. It does not shape conduct: it is itself the exemplification of a particular way of looking at life. A concert is not a sermon. It is a performance — a reincarnation of a series of ideas implicit in the work of art.

As a composer and a musical citizen I am concerned with one more problem of the gifted listener: one that is special to our own period. Despite the attractions of phonograph and radio, which are considerable, true music-lovers insist on hearing live performances of music. An unusual and disturbing situation has gradually become all-pervasive at public performances of music: the universal preponderance of old music on concert programs.

This unhealthy state of affairs, this obsession with old music, tends to make all music listening safe and unadventurous since it deals so largely in the works of the accepted masters. Filling our halls with familiar sounds induces a sense of security in our audiences; they are gradually losing all need to exercise freely their own musical judgment. Over and over again the same limited number of bona fide, guaranteed masterpieces are on display; by inference, therefore, it is mainly these works that are worth our notice. This narrows considerably in the minds of a broad public the very conception of how varied musical experience may be, and puts all lesser works in a false light. It conventionalizes programs, obviously, and overemphasizes the interpreter's role, for only through seeking out new "readings" is it possible to repeat the same works year after year. Most pernicious of all, it leaves a bare minimum of wall space for the showing of the works of new composers, without which the supply of future writers of masterworks is certain to dry up.

This state of affairs is not merely a local or national one — it pervades the musical life of every country that professes love for western music. Nine-tenths of the time a program performed in a concert hall in Buenos Aires provides an exact replica of what goes on in a concert hall of London or of Tel-Aviv. Music is no longer merely an international language, it is an international commodity.

This concentration on masterworks is having a profound influence on present-day musical life. A solemn wall of respectability surrounds the haloed masterpieces of music and deadens their impact. They are written about too often out of a sticky sentiment steeped in conventionality. It is both exhilarating and depressing to think of them: exhilarating to think that great masses of people are put in daily contact with them, have the possibility of truly taking sustenance from them; and depressing to watch these same classics used to snuff out all liveliness, all immediacy from the contemporary musical scene.

Reverence for the classics in our time has been turned into a form of discrimination against all other music. Professor Edward Dent spoke his mind on this same subject when he came to the United States in 1936 to accept an honorary doctorate from Harvard University. Reverence for the classics, in his opinion, was traceable to the setting up of a "religion of music," intrinsic to the ideas of Beethoven and promulgated by Richard Wagner. "In the days of Handel and Mozart," he said, "nobody wanted old music; all audiences demanded the newest opera or the newest concerto, as we now naturally demand the newest play and the newest novel. If in those two branches of imaginative production we habitually demand the newest and the latest, why is it that in music we almost invariably demand what is old-fashioned and out of date, while the music of the present day is often received with positive hostility." "All music, even church music," he added, "was 'utility music,' music for the particular moment."

This situation, remarked upon fifteen years ago by Professor Dent, is now intensified through the role played by commercial interests in the purveying of music. Professor Dent was himself aware of that fact, for he pointed out then that "the religious outlook on music is an affair of business as well as of devotion." The big public is now frightened of investing in any music that doesn't have the label "masterwork" stamped on it. Thus along with the classics themselves we are given the "light classics," the "jazz classics," and even "modern classics." Radio programs, record advertisements, adult appreciation courses — all focus attention on a restricted list of the musical great in such a way that there appears to be no other *raison d'être* for music. In the same way musical references in books harp upon the names of a few musical giants. The final irony is that the people who are persuaded to concern themselves only with the best in music are the very ones who would have most difficulty in recognizing a real masterpiece when they heard one.

The simple truth is that our concert halls have been turned into musical museums — auditory museums of a most limited kind. Our musical era is sick in that respect — our composers invalids who exist on the fringe of musical society, and our listeners impoverished through a relentless repetition of the same works signed by a handful of sanctified names.

Our immediate concern is the effect all this has on the listener of unusual gifts. A narrow and limited repertoire in the concert hall results in a narrow and limited musical experience. No true musical enthusiast wants to be confined to a few hundred years of musical history. He naturally seeks out every type of musical experience; his intuitive understanding gives him a sense of assurance whether he is confronted with the recently deciphered treasures of Gothic art, or the quick wit of a Chabrier or a Bizet, or the latest importation of Italian dodecaphonism. A healthy musical curiosity and a broad musical experience sharpens the critical faculty of even the most talented amateur.

All this has bearing on our relation to the classic masters also. To listen to music in a familiar style and to listen freshly, ignoring what others have said or written and testing its values for oneself, is a mark of the intelligent listener. The classics themselves must be reinterpreted in terms of our own period if we are to hear them anew and "keep their perennial humanity living and capable of assimilation." But in order to do that, we must have a balanced musical diet that permits us to set off our appraisals of the old masters against the varied and different musical manifestations of more recent times. For it is only in the light of the whole musical experience that the classics become most meaningful.

The dream of every musician who loves his art is to involve gifted listeners everywhere as an active force in the musical community. The attitude of each individual listener, especially the gifted listener, is the principal resource we have in bringing to fruition the immense musical potentialities of our own time.

CHAPTER TWO

The Sonorous Image

ONE OF THE PRIME CONCERNS in the making of music, either as creator or as interpreter, is the question how it will sound. On any level, whether the music is abstruse and absolute or whether it is intended for the merest diversion, it has got to "sound." The worst reproach you can make against a composer is to tell him that what he has written is "paper music." On the other hand, one of the quickest ways to recognize talent in the youthful composer is to note the natural effectiveness as sound of even the most casual combination of different tone colors. It is a sure sign of inborn musicality. The way music sounds, or the sonorous image, as I call it, is nothing more than an auditory concept that floats in the mind of the executant or composer; a prethinking of the exact nature of the tones to be produced.

Let me tell you of a little incident that illustrates the importance of "sound" from a musician's standpoint. A few years ago I happened to be in the NBC Radio City studios on business. On my way out I passed by Studio 8H, and hearing a distant music, I realized that a rehearsal of the NBC Symphony was in progress. By peeking through the glass partition of the door I was able to recognize a famous conductor and a famous soloist in the midst of rehearsing a concerto. My curiosity got the better of me, and I decided to stop by for a short time and see how things were going. With the exaggerated care of an uninvited guest I slipped quietly into an orchestra seat at the center rear of the auditorium. As far as I could tell I was alone; no one had seen me come in. That was lucky, for otherwise I might very well have been unceremoniously ejected. Soloist, conductor, and orchestra were in the thick of it, entirely absorbed with the work in hand. I was there no more than five minutes before the familiar moment arrived; I mean that moment in any concerto when the solo performer reaches a high point and pauses as the orchestral accompaniment sweeps forward in ever-mounting passion. At that instant, without warning, the soloist leaped from the platform and headed straight down the center aisle in my direction. I immediately thought: he doesn't want me here, spying on his rehearsal in this way. But before I could make a move he was upon me. Perspiring and out of breath he fairly shouted at me: "Aaron, how does it sound?" Before I could utter a word in reply he was gone in order to reach the stage in time for his next entrance.

Yes, the sonorous image is a preoccupying concern of all musicians. In that phrase we include beauty and roundness of tone; its warmth, its depth, its "edge," its balanced mixture with other tones, and its acoustical properties in any given environment. The creation of a satisfactory aural image is not merely a matter of musical talent or technical adroitness; imagination plays a large role here. You cannot produce a beautiful sonority or combination of sonorities without first hearing the imagined sound in the inner ear. Once this imagined sonority is heard in reality, it impresses itself unforgettably on the mind. To this day I can remember with extreme vividness the morning in 1925 when I heard sounding for the first time a work of my own orchestration. For some reason I was late to the rehearsal so that my music was in progress when I arrived at the hall. It excited me so that I was afraid I was literally about to fall over. More than once I have gone backstage to speak with the conductor after he has given a first reading to a new orchestral work of mine in order to discuss changes in balance or interpretation. Often these changes have to do with minute details that depend upon a precise memory of what was heard for only a passing instant at the rehearsal. Neither the conductor nor myself, nor any other composer for that matter, would find this feat unusual. The impact of sheer sound on the musician's psyche is so familiar an idea that we tend to take for granted the force it represents.

Most people's aural memory is remarkably strong; heard sounds remain in the mind for long periods of time, and with a sharpness that is also remarkable. From the early twenties I still retain an impression of fantastic sonorities after a first contact with Schönberg's *Pierrot Lunaire,* or a little later, the astonishing percussive imaginings of Edgar Varèse, especially in a piece called *Arcanes,* heard once but not again. Also from the early twenties I recall hearing the mysterious sound made by a string ensemble in an adjoining hotel room in Salzburg, a sound which was later identified as an Alois Hába quarter tone *Quartet.* For me the important thing was not the quarter tones, but the sonorous image that was left with me. I can remember too the particular acid sound of a Mexican small-town band playing in the public square on Sunday mornings in Tlaxcala. Were they playing out of tune, do you think? Perhaps, but nevertheless they were creating an aural image authentically their own. So was an English choir of boys and men's voices that I heard in a London cathedral. They had a hollow, an almost cadaverous quality; not pretty, perhaps, but certainly memorable. Most unforgettable sound of all was that of a massed orchestra and band of some one thousand high school performers in an Atlantic City convention hall all simultaneously searching for the note *A.* It is hopeless to attempt to describe that sound. Jericho's walls must have heard some such unearthly musical noise.

I do not mean to suggest that sounds in themselves, taken out of context, are of any use to a composer. Interesting sonorities as such are scarcely more than icing on the musical cake. But a deliberately chosen sound image that pervades an entire piece becomes an in-

23

tegral part of the expressive meaning of that piece. One thinks immediately of the two different versions that Stravinsky tells us he made of his ballet *Les Noces* before deciding upon a third and final solution: the unusual combination of four pianos and thirteen percussion players. The rarefied timbres of Anton Webern's little string quartet pieces would be meaningless if transcribed for any other medium. In contrast with this are the original effects obtained from the most ordinary means: for example, the juxtaposition of a loud and vigorous body of strings against a soft and undulant pair of harps in Britten's *Spring Symphony* — once heard it cannot successfully be rethought for any other combination.

The ability to imagine sounds in advance of their being heard in actuality is one factor that widely separates the professional from the layman. Professionals themselves are unevenly gifted in this respect. More than one celebrated composer has struggled to produce an adequate orchestral scoring of his own music. Certain performers, on the other hand, seem especially gifted in being able to call forth delicious sonorities from their instrument. The layman's capacity for imagining unheard sound images seems, by and large, to be rather poor. This does not apply on the lowest plane of sound apprehension where, of course, there is no difficulty. Laboratory tests have demonstrated that differences in tone color are the first differences apparent to the untrained ear. Any child is capable of distinguishing the sound of a human voice from the sound of a violin. The contrast between a voice and its echo is apparent to everyone. But it bespeaks a fair degree of musical sophistication to be able to distinguish the sound of an oboe from that of an English horn, and a marked degree to imagine a whole group of wood winds sounding together. If you have ever had occasion, as I have, to perform an orchestral score on the piano to a group of nonprofessionals, you will have soon realized how little sense they have of how this music might be expected to sound in an orchestra.

It is surprising to note how little investigation has been devoted to this whole sphere of music. There are no textbooks solely designed to examine the sound stuff of music — the history of its past by comparison with its present; or its future; or its potential. Even so-called orchestration texts, written ostensibly to describe the science of combining orchestral instruments, are generally found to steer shy of their subject, concentrating instead on instrumentation, that is, on the examination of the technical and tonal possibilities of the individual instrument. The sonorous image appears to be a kind of aural mirage, not easily immobilized and analyzed. The case of the individual sound is rather different since it is more comparable to that of the primary colors in painting. It is the full spectrum of the musician's "color" palette that seems to lend itself much less well to discussion and consideration than that of the painter.

There are many diverse and interesting questions concerning the role of tone color, or sound image, in musical thinking. My contention that tonal image and expressive meaning are inter-connected in the composer's mind is more true today than it was in the past, if I read my history books correctly. In the eighteenth century music was meant to be played — that was the first consideration. What instruments it was played by seems often to have been dictated by the requirements of a particular occasion. Bach's arrangements of other men's works, and Mozart's alterations in a Handel score are paralleled, in the following century, by Liszt's piano versions of Schubert's songs. Nowadays we tend to look upon transcriptions with suspicion because we consider the composer's expressive idea to be reflected in a precise way by its tonal investiture. We go even further: we assume that the choice of the sound medium itself will almost certainly influence the nature of the composer's thought, as witness some of the examples I have already mentioned.

Thought and sound can interact one upon the other only insofar as the composer or executant is sensitive to the medium adopted. The remarkable affinity of certain composers for certain sound media has been pointed out many times, but not the corresponding limitation that sometimes accompanies this affinity. The most famous example, is, of course, Chopin's extraordinary felicity in writing for the piano. Suppose he had been born into a world before the invention of the piano, what would have happened to his composing talent in that case? I frankly don't know. I do know that his friends tried over and over again to persuade him to broaden his tonal range, without success. His reply, as we have it in a letter, was as follows: "I know my limitations, and I know I'd make a fool of myself if I tried to climb too high without having the ability to do it. They plague me to death urging me to write symphonies and operas, and they want me to be everything in one, a Polish Rossini and a Mozart and a Beethoven. But I just laugh under my breath and think to myself that one must start from small things. I'm only a pianist, and if I'm worth anything this is good too . . . I think it's better to do only a little but to do that as well as possible, rather than try to do all things and do them poorly."

We think of the younger Scarlatti as an analogous case because of his genius for the harpsichord; and history shows many other examples of the sympathy of certain composers for specific media: Hugo Wolf for the solo voice, Ravel for the harp, and Brahms for the small chamber music ensemble. And what of the masters of the nineteenth century orchestra — Berlioz, Wagner, and Richard Strauss — is it mere chance that they have no piano music to speak of? Or that Debussy composed but seldom for unaccompanied chorus and Fauré seldom for the orchestra? From these few examples it would appear that expressive purpose is closely allied to specific sound media, quite different in the case of different composers.

To a considerable degree, of course, sound images are imposed upon us from without. We are born to certain inherited sounds and tend to take them for granted. Other peoples, however, have an absorbing interest in quite different kinds of auditory materials. The Orient, for instance, leaves us far behind in sensitivity to the subtle variety of percussive sounds. Dr. Curt Sachs, in writing on oriental music, mentions the "dizzying mass of wooden, bamboo, stone, glass, porcelain, and metal implements, to be pounded, shaken, rubbed or struck." Our own poverty-stricken percussive imaginings are put to shame by comparison with the richness and diversity and delicacy of the oriental mind in this connection. One wonders what the comparatively undifferentiated sonority of a string quartet might communicate to a Balinese musician, brought up on the clangorously varied sonorities of a gamelan. On the other hand the complex harmonic textures obtainable from our keyboard instruments are a closed book to the Eastern musician. Dr. Sachs tells us that an Arab, given a piano, plays in "empty octaves" and the Hindus, "in single, sustained notes on the harmonium."

It is clear, then, that musicians of the East and the West are both restricted by birth to a comparatively limited gamut of inherited sound materials. Perhaps this is just as well; otherwise we might be overwhelmed by the too numerous attractions of tonal color possibilities. Western musical history is characterized, moreover, by the identification of specific sound media with certain periods, to the practical exclusion of other possible sound media, and it was because of this exclusive interest that the medium chosen could be developed so highly. The cultivation of music for voices, especially choral music, up to about the year 1600 is a prime example. Virgil Thomson once told me ruefully that he thought composers of that time were so wonderfully adept at exploiting the possibilities of the human voice in choral combination that they had left practically nothing really new for us to do in that medium as far as exceptional effects are concerned. The exhaustion of any medium forces composers in other directions; this undoubtedly was partly the reason for the development of interest in purely instrumental writing during the period that followed the choral age. A further enrichment in the way of tonal combinations came with the joining of the large choral mass with orchestra, as in the oratorios of Handel. The nineteenth century, less fascinated by the choral medium, concentrated on the new sounds of the quickly developing, self-sufficient symphony orchestra. We are still occupied with that task. But in addition, our own period has shown a preoccupation with sonorities that do not depend upon string tone as its principal ingredient. A new emphasis on wood wind and brass sonorities, with their drier, less sentimental connotations, is characteristic of our time. I mention this in passing as merely one instance of choice being exercised in respect to felicitous sound materials.

Thus far I have tried to suggest the musician's concern with the sonorous image; the endless variety of possible sound combinations; the changing situation with regard to sound media; and the limited use by composers of different sonorous potentials, either through lack of imagination or through inherited conceptions of desirable sound.

Now let us look a little more closely at the sonorous means at the disposal of the composer in terms of the single instrument. Here again the composer is far from being a free agent; he is hedged about with limitations — limitations in the manufacture of the performing machine (for that is what an instrument is), and limitations in the technical proficiency of the performer who uses the machine. Sometimes in moments of impatience such as every creator must have, I have imagined the sweeping away overnight of all our known instruments through the invention of new electronic devices that would end the constraints within which we work by providing us with instruments that would present no problem of pitch, duration, intensity, or speed. As it is, we must always keep in mind that every string, every wood wind and brass can play only so high and so low, only so fast and so slow, only so loud and so soft; not forgetting the famous matter of "breath-control" for the wind players that is defied at one's peril. No wonder Beethoven is reported to have said, when he heard that his violinist friend Schuppanzigh was complaining about the unplayability of his part: "That he should think of his miserable fiddle, when the spirit is speaking in me!"

Yes, composers struggle with their instruments — and not infrequently with their instrumentalists. Yet despite restrictions imposed by necessity, they do not view this entirely as a hardship. In fact, in certain circumstances the discipline enforced by the limitations of an instrument or a performer acts as a spur to the composer's imagination. Once, during a visit to Bahia in Brazil, it occurred to me that I wouldn't at all mind composing for one of their native instruments called the berimbau. The berimbau has but one string, on which the player produces only two tones, a whole tone apart. It isn't played with a bow, it is struck by a small wooden stick. The trick that gives it fascination is a wooden shell, open at one end, which is held against the string and reflects the sound in the manner of an echo chamber. At the same time, the hand that wields the stick jiggles a kind of rattle. When several berimbau players are heard together they set up a sweetly jangled tinkle which I found completely absorbing. I felt confident that if I had to, I could compose something for the berimbau that would hold the listener's attention despite the very limited tonal range it affords. This confidence in the handling of instruments and this natural accommodation to the limitations of any instrument is the composer's stock in trade.

The principal concern of the composer is to seek out the expressive nature of any particular instrument and write with that in mind. There is that music which belongs in the flute and only in the flute. A certain objective lyricism, a kind of ethereal fluidity we connect with the flute. Composers of imagination have broadened our conceptions of what was possible on a particular instrument, but beyond a certain point, defined by the nature of the instrument itself, even the most gifted composer cannot go.

Think of what Liszt did for the piano. No other composer before him — not even Chopin — better understood how to manipulate the keyboard of the piano so as to produce the most satisfying sound textures ranging from the comparative simplicity of a beautifully spaced accompanimental figure to the shimmering of a delicate cascade of chords. One might argue that this emphasis upon the sound-appeal of music weakens its spiritual and ethical qualities. But even so, one cannot deny the role of pioneer to Liszt in this regard, for without his sensuously contrived pieces we would not have had the loveliness of Debussy's or Ravel's textures, and certainly not the languorous piano poems of Alexandre Scriabin. Liszt quite simply transformed the piano, bringing out not only its own inherent qualities, but its evocative nature as well: the piano as orchestra, the piano as harp, the piano as cembalum, the piano as organ, as brass choir, even the percussive piano as we know it may be traced to Liszt's incomparable handling of the instrument. His pieces were born *in* the piano, so to speak; they could never have been written at a table.

Combinations of a few instruments in chamber music ensembles have tended toward conventional groupings over the years. The most usual groups combine instruments of the same family: thus we have string trios, quartets, quintets, sextets, and so forth; and wood-wind groupings of an analogous kind. The piano, because of its very different sound, has always been a problem when added to any of these groups but not an insuperable one when carefully handled — and, one should add, expertly played.

Our own period has tried to break the monotony of the usual groupings by combining instruments in a fresh way. I might choose at random examples of imaginary groupings such as viola, saxophone, and harp, or two violins, flute, and vibraphone; or quote actual combinations from Bartók such as the music for two pianos and two percussionists, or the *Contrasts* for violin, clarinet, and piano. Musical literature would supply numerous other examples. Perhaps the early jazz band had some part in this stimulation of interest in unusual ensembles. At any rate, the first arrival in Europe, around 1918, of American jazz was followed by a wave of interest in chamber orchestra and chamber opera, with emphasis on new tonal experiments. Stravinsky's *Histoire du Soldat* was such a work and so was

Milhaud's *La Création du Monde*. Manuel de Falla's Harpsichord Concerto dates from the same period, and in its modest contrast of two strings and three wood winds against the newly revived harpsichord tone, we get an offshoot of the new sonorous vitality and a new tonal landscape.

The apex of sonorous imaginativeness in our period is generally conceded to be the ability to compose for the many-voiced concord of the symphony orchestra — the "grand" orchestra, it used to be called. There is a natural curiosity on the part of the layman to want to know how precise a composer's orchestral imagination is. "Can you tell in advance *exactly* how your orchestration will sound" is a question I am often asked. The answer is that it partly depends on how adventurous you are. If the composer is satisfied with a sure-fire kind of orchestration limited to tested effects, then certainly a fairly precise result can be predicted. It's the calculated risk of an unusual combination that makes orchestral results uncertain at times. But a truly brilliant orchestrator, it would seem to me, must take chances. Musical history recounts many instances of composers making adjustments in their scores after having heard how they sound, in order to approximate more closely the imagined effect; and these instances concern even those whom we know to be masters of the orchestra. Arnold Schönberg reported that Richard Strauss showed him several cases where changes had to be made, and he added: "I know that Gustav Mahler had to change his orchestration very much for the sake of transparency."

One of the principal reasons for this uncertainty in the mixing of tones comes from the fact that each individual tone that we hear is accompanied by a series of partials or overtones. These partials, unheard by most of us, nevertheless do affect the way in which tones combine. That too makes the acoustical engineer's job a precarious one. In spite of his careful measurements of decibels and frequencies there is still no guarantee that he can design the perfect concert-hall. The mixing of sonant vibrations is by definition a hazardous undertaking. For the composer there are additional hazards in the variety of tone produced by different players, the size and acoustical properties of the auditorium, and the talent of the conductor who supposedly controls the relative dynamic balance of the combined instrumental body.

Nevertheless, and despite these difficulties, it is quite possible to describe the basic requirements of a good orchestrator. It is axiomatic that no one can satisfactorily orchestrate music which was not conceived in orchestral terms in the first place. The music must, by its nature, belong to the orchestra, so to speak, even before one can tell in exactly what kind of orchestral dress it will appear. Assuming that one does have orchestratable music, what governs the choice of instruments? Nothing but the composer's expressive purpose. And how does one give expressive purpose through orchestral color? Through the choice of those timbres, or combination of timbres, that have closest emotional connotation with one's expressive idea.

The modern orchestra has at its command an enormous wealth of color combinations. It is this *embarras de richesses* that has proved the undoing of the typical commercial radio or movie orchestrator. Where there is no true expressive purpose anything goes; in fact, everything goes, and it all goes into the same piece. The so-called Hollywood orchestration is a composite of all the known tricks in the orchestrator's bag. Stephen Spender points out a like situation with regard to poets "who allow their imaginations to lead them into a pleasant garden of poetic phrases" and contrasts them with "those who use language as an instrument to hew a replica of their experience into words." The situation is similar in music; composers must not allow their imagination to lead them into a pleasant garden of orchestral effects; it is the expressive idea that dictates to the composer the nature of his orchestral sound, and supplies a discipline against the *nouveau riche* temptations of the modern orchestra.

But even when the composer's expressive purpose is clearly before him there appear to be two different approaches to the problem of orchestration: one is to "think in color" at the very moment of composition, the other is to "choose color" after a sketch of the work is at hand. Most composers of my acquaintance make a virtue of the first system; that is, they claim to think coloristically. A feat is, of course, implied. If, at the instant the composer conceives a melody, he at the same instant knows what its orchestral dress will be, he has performed two operations simultaneously. Some few composers have told me that they prepare no sketch; they compose directly into score, thinking the timbre and the notes together. It seems to me, however, that there are definite advantages to be gained from separating these two functions. The method of choosing colors only at the moment that one begins deliberately to orchestrate makes it possible to plan out an entire score in terms of its over-all effect. It counteracts the tendency to orchestrate page by page which is certain to lead to poor results, for the decisions made on any single page are valid only in relation to what has gone before and what is to follow. Since balance and contrast of instrumental effect are prime factors in good orchestration, it follows that any decision as to timbre, too quickly arrived at, is itself a limitation, since it prevents freedom of action on other pages. This greater freedom of choice, it would appear, is possible only if the composer deliberately prevents himself from thinking in color until the moment comes for applying himself solely to that purpose. This isn't always possible, for there are times when a phrase or a section suggests its orchestral form so forcibly as not to be ignored. These moments, when they really impose themselves, act as a catalytic in the general orchestral scheme. But in general I belong to the category of instrumentator whose orchestral framework and detail is carefully planned so as to carry out more faithfully the expressive purpose inherent in the entirely completed ground plan of the work. If I stress this unduly it is only to counteract what is generally supposed to be normal procedure in orchestration.

Thus far I have been discussing general principles of orchestral

technique. Now I should like to examine orchestral ideals as we find
them exemplified in the works of different composers at different
periods of musical history. The story of the orchestra as we think
of it (and apart from its early connection with opera) begins comparatively late, after 1750 certainly, when composers began to mark
their scores so as to indicate precisely what instruments were to
play what notes. Until that happened, sounds were more or less
improvised according to the players available, which naturally varied
considerably in different times and places. Because the composer was
so frequently involved in the performance himself as instrumentalist,
we can conclude that the orchestral sounds that were made fully
mirrored his wishes, but since these were not indicated in printed
scores it leaves us with only a hazy notion of the sonorities produced.
By the latter part of the eighteenth century the basis for what was
later to be developed into our modern orchestras was established.
The constitution of the orchestra at that time was the body of strings,
with plain juxtapositions of a few wood winds and some brass. These
latter instruments, especially, were limited in the part they could
play by deficiencies in manufacture and the technical limitations of
the players. Therefore, no great problem of orchestral effect was in
question. Each instrument was used frankly for its own sound, so
that an oboe sounded like an oboe and a bassoon like a bassoon. A
more imaginative application of the same principles may be observed
in the scores of Haydn and Mozart. Here a delightful clarity of
texture was obtained by showing off in their most grateful registers
the natural characteristics of each instrument. This was the age of
innocence in orchestration.

With Beethoven some of the problems of modern orchestration
were faced for the first time. He had a larger and more complex
body of instruments at his command and produced a rugged and
honest sound, a sound without much finesse or subtlety of effect,
from our vantage point, perhaps, but one that somehow adequately

clothes the music of the symphonies and overtures. Still he left much to be done in that field.

It is generally agreed that it was the orchestral genius of Hector Berlioz that was responsible for the invention of the modern orchestra as we think of it. Up to his time composers used instruments in order to make them sound like themselves; the mixing of colors so as to produce a new result was his achievement. Berlioz took advantage of the ambiguity of timbre that each instrument has in varying degrees, and thereby introduced the element of orchestral magic as a contemporary composer would understand it. The brilliance of his orchestration comes partly by way of this ability to *blend* instruments — not merely to keep them out of one another's way. His skillful writing for the individual instruments disclosed the unsuspected characteristics of their different registers. The particular registers chosen for each group of instruments enhances the sheen and sparkle of the combined texture. Add to this his incredible daring in forcing instrumentalists to play better than they knew they could play. He paid the price, no doubt, in hearing his music inadequately performed. But imagine the excitement of hearing in one's inner ear sonorities that had never before been set down by any other man. It is the subtle calculation of these masterly scores that convinces me that Berlioz was more, much more, than the starry-eyed romantic of the history books.

It would be easy to point to specific examples of Berlioz' orchestral daring. The use of the double basses in four-part pizzicati at the beginning of the March to the Scaffold from the *Symphonie Fantastique,* the writing for four tympani, also in chordal style, at the conclusion of the movement that precedes the March; the use of English horn and piccolo clarinet to typify pastoral and devilish sentiments, respectively; the gossamer texture of Queen Mab with its Debussian harps and high antique cymbals; the sensitive mixtures of low flutes with string tone at the beginning of the Love

35

Scene from *Romeo* — these and numerous other examples prove that Berlioz brought to music an uncanny instinct for orchestral wizardry.

The lessons to be learned from Berlioz were incorporated into the later scores of Wagner and Strauss. Wagner's orchestration was always effective and sometimes startlingly original, but nevertheless a heavy German sauce seems to have covered what was once a Gallic base. The primary colors used by earlier and later orchestrators are comparatively little in evidence, and instead a continual doubling of one instrument with another produces an overall neutral fatness of sound which has lost all differentiation and distinction. Strauss, who had edited the well-known Berlioz treatise on instrumentation, continued the Wagnerian orchestral tradition, adding a special brilliance of his own. The scoring of his symphonic poems composed around the beginning of the century left our elders breathless. They remain breath-taking in one sense, that is, if one examines them on the printed page and appreciates the mental ingenuity and musical knowledge they represent. But as sheer sound they have lost much of the compelling force they once had, for they seem over-elaborate and unnecessarily cluttered with a hundred ingenious details that are not heard as such in performance, and produce in the end an orchestral sonority not so very different from that of a bloated Wagnerism. Reservations should be made, however, for Strauss's finest orchestral pages, such as those in *Salome* or *Electra,* which are prophetic of what was to follow.

It was the Russian school of composers — especially Tchaikovsky and Rimsky-Korsakoff — who were most directly influenced by the Berlioz scores. Rimsky wrote the textbook on orchestration that was the "bible" of our student days. Although the advice he gave was solid enough, it turned out to be of only limited application, for it assumed that the elements of harmony, melody, and figuration would retain the same relative positions of importance that they have in a Rimsky-Korsakoff score. But our scores are likely to be more contrapuntally conceived than Rimsky-Korsakoff's; therefore his good advice—a bit too schematic in the first place—has become less and less serviceable.

Moreover, a completely new conception of delicacy and magic in orchestral coloring had been introduced in France during the early twentieth century. The scores of Debussy and Ravel not only looked different on the page, they sounded different in the orchestra. What a pity that Ravel never wrote a treatise on orchestration! The first precept would have been: no doubling allowed, except in the full orchestral *tutti*. In other words, discover again the purity of the individual hue. And when you mix your pure colors be sure to mix them with exactitude, for only in that way can you hope to obtain the optimum of delicate or dazzling timbres. An instinctual knowledge of the potentiality of each instrument plus a balanced calculation of their combined effect helps to explain, in part, the orchestral delights of the later Ravel scores. Debussy, by comparison, was less precise in his orchestral workmanship, depending on his personal sensitivity for obtaining subtle balances, and as a consequence his scores need careful adjustment on the part of orchestra and conductor.

Musical impressionism was superseded by the arrival in Paris in 1910 of a new master of the orchestra: Igor Stravinsky. *The Fire Bird* showed what he could do under the influence of the Rimsky-Ravel color scheme. But in the two ballets that followed, Stravinsky hit his stride: *Petrouchka* had no rivals for brilliance and exhilaration of orchestral effect; and *Le Sacre du Printemps* remains, after forty years, the most astonishing orchestral achievement of the twentieth century. We must not underestimate the importance of the new rhythms and polytonal harmonies in the creation of this amazing orchestral sound. But for the most part it depends upon an unprecedented degree of virtuosity in the marshaling of orchestral forces. The pitting of energized strings and piercing wood winds against the sharp cutting edge of brass, the whole underlined by an

37

explosive percussive wallop, typifies *Le Sacre,* and inaugurates a new era in orchestral practice.

Ten years later it was an entirely different sound-ideal that held Stravinsky's interest. In place of brilliance, the neoclassic works emphasized the dry sonorities of wind ensembles without the string tone added — the grays and browns of a new and more sober color scheme. Later, in the ballets of *Apollo* and *Orpheus,* Stravinsky evinced renewed interest in the strings and gave them a texture all his own; especially the string tone of *Orpheus* glows with a rich, dark hue. No other composer has ever shown greater awareness of the natural correlation of tonal image with expressive content.

In briefly reviewing the picture of modern orchestration one ought not fail to mention the influence of that remarkable conductor-composer Gustav Mahler. The orchestral *trouvailles* of his nine symphonies were highly suggestive to composers like Schönberg and Alban Berg, as well as to the later generation of Honegger, Shostakovitch, and Benjamin Britten. Mahler, despite the deeply romantic substance of his music, composed in long and independent melodic lines, not unrelated to the baroque contrapuntal textures of eighteenth-century composers. Scoring these for an orchestra that had no need for "filling in" harmonies of the nineteenth century, and avoiding as far as posisble all use of orchestral "pedaling" effects, Mahler achieved an instrumental clarity that had no model in his time. The clear contrapuntal lines, and the sharp juxtapositions of one orchestral section against another — strings against brass, for instance — as we find it in the scores of Hindemith or Roy Harris are traceable to Mahler's influence. Schönberg was especially insistent about his debt to Mahler. The use of the orchestra as if it were a large ensemble of chamber music players, with the notion of giving each tone in the harmonic complex its solo color was a Schönberg derivation by way of Mahler. These are but a few of the results Mahler's orchestral mastery has had on the composers of our own time.

The sonorous image-ideal of the future — even the immediate

future — seems highly conjectural. In a supersonic age the material of sound itself is likely to become less ethereal and ephemeral, more solidly tangible. Carlos Chavez once envisaged a collaboration of musicians and engineers that would produce, as he put it, "a material appropriate and practical for huge electric musical performances." He goes on to imagine a perfect gradation of coloring through an incredible variety of timbres; and increased perspective of sound through more subtle intensities. The possibilities are endless; the probabilities are that something radical is in the making.

The sound-wave instruments of Theremin and Martenot, the electronic organ, the ability to write music directly on film, the experimentations with noise as a musical ingredient in sound films and in the scores of the French composers of the new *musique concrète* — all these and other similar manifestations seem to point to wide horizons of new sound images. But just as in the past, it is perhaps comforting to remember, we, the composers, are the ones who must give meaning to whatever sonorous images the engineers can invent.

CHAPTER THREE

The Creative Mind
and the Interpretative Mind

IN THE ART OF MUSIC, creation and interpretation are indissolubly linked, more so than in any of the other arts, with the possible exception of dancing. Both these activities — creation and interpretation — demand an imaginative mind — that is self-evident. Both bring into play creative energies that are sometimes alike, sometimes dissimilar. By coupling them together it may be possible to illuminate their relationship and their interaction, one upon the other.

Like most creative artists, I have from time to time cogitated on the mysterious nature of creativity. Is there anything new to be said about the creative act — anything really new, I mean? I rather doubt it. The idea of creative man goes back so far in time, so many cogent things have been written and said — acute observations, poetic reflections, and philosophic ponderings, that one despairs of bringing to the subject anything more than a private view of an immense terrain.

Still, the serious composer who thinks about his art will sooner or later have occasion to ask himself: why is it so important to my own psyche that I compose music? What makes it seem so absolutely necessary, so that every other daily activity, by comparison, is of lesser significance? And why is the creative impulse never satisfied;

why must one always begin anew? To the first question — the need to create — the answer is always the same — self-expression; the basic need to make evident one's deepest feelings about life. But why is the job never done? Why must one always begin again? The reason for the compulsion to renewed creativity, it seems to me, is that each added work brings with it an element of self-discovery. I must create in order to know myself, and since self-knowledge is a never-ending search, each new work is only a part-answer to the question "Who am I?" and brings with it the need to go on to other and different part-answers. Because of this, each artist's work is supremely important — at least to himself. But why does the artist presume to think, and why do other men encourage him to think, that the creation of one more work of art is of more than merely private import? That is because each new and significant work of art is a unique formulation of experience; an experience that would be utterly lost if it were not captured and set down by the artist. No other artist will ever make that particular formulation in exactly that way. And just as the individual creator discovers himself through his creation, so the world at large knows itself through its artists, discovers the very nature of its Being through the creations of its artists.

Jacques Maritain has summarized this idea of the necessity and uniqueness of the work of art in these terms: it is the artist's condition, he says, "to seize obscurely his own being with a knowledge that will not come to anything, save in being creative, and which will not be conceptualized save in a work made by his own hands." Thus the creator finds himself in a precarious position because, first, the involuntary nature of creation makes the moment of engendering an art work uncertain, and then, once conceived, there comes the fear that the conception may not be brought to fruition. This gives a dramatic aspect to the composer's situation. On the one hand the need for self-expression is ever-present, but on the other hand, he cannot, by an act of will, produce the work of art. It must either be

41

entirely spontaneous, or if not spontaneous, then cajoled, induced, gradually perceived — so that each day's work may spell failure or triumph. No wonder many creative artists have been reputed to have had unstable characters.

Up to this point, the situation of the musical interpreter is not so very different from that of the creator. He is simply the intermediary that brings the composer's work to life — a kind of midwife to the composition. He partakes of the same dedication of purpose, the same sense of self-discovery through each performance, the same conviction that something unique is lost, possibly, when his own understanding of a work of art is lost. He even partakes of the involuntary nature of creation, for we know that he cannot at will turn on the wellsprings of his creativity so that each performance may be of equal value. Quite the contrary, each time he steps out upon the concert platform we wish him luck, for he shares something of the creator's uncertain powers of projection. Thus we see that interpretation, even though it may rightfully be thought of as an auxiliary art, does share elements of creativity with the mind that forms the work of art.

But now let us consider the essential way in which creation and interpretation are radically different. The interpretative mind can exercise itself on a given object; it cannot itself supply that object. The making of something out of nothing is the special province of the creative mind. The composer is a kind of magician; out of the recesses of his thought he produces, or finds himself in possession of, the generative idea. Although I say "the recesses of his thought," in actuality the source of the germinal idea is the one phase in creation that resists rational explanation. All we know is that the moment of possession is the moment of inspiration; or to use Coleridge's phrase, the moment when the creator is in "a more than usual state of emotion." Whence it comes, or in what manner it comes, or how long its duration one can never foretell. Inspiration may be a form of superconsciousness, or perhaps of subconsciousness — I wouldn't

42

know; but I am sure that it is the antithesis of self-consciousness. The inspired moment may sometimes be described as a kind of hallucinatory state of mind: one half of the personality emotes and dictates while the other half listens and notates. The half that listens had better look the other way, had better simulate a half attention only, for the half that dictates is easily disgruntled and avenges itself for too close inspection by fading entirely away.

That describes, of course, only one kind of inspiration. Another kind involves the personality as a whole, or rather, loses sight of it completely, in a spontaneous expression of emotional release. By that I mean the creative impulse takes possession in a way that blots out in greater or lesser degree consciousness of the familiar sort. Both these types of inspiration — if one can call them types — are generally of brief duration and of exhausting effect. They are the rarer kind, the kind we wait for every day. The less divine afflatus that makes it possible for us to compose each day — to induce inspiration, as it were — is a species of creative intuition in which the critical faculty is much more involved. But I shall come to that in a moment. Long works need intuitiveness of that sort, for it is generally the shorter ones that are entirely the result of spontaneous creativity.

Mere length in music is central to the composer's problem. To write a three-minute piece is not difficult; a main section, a contrasting section, and a return to the first part is the usual solution. But anything that lasts beyond three minutes may cause trouble. In treating so amorphous a material as music the composer is confronted with this principal problem: how to extend successfully the seminal ideas and how to shape the whole so that it adds up to a rounded experience. Here, too, inspiration of a kind is needed. No textbook rules can be applied, for the simple reason that these generative ideas are themselves live things and demand their individual treatment. I have sometimes wondered whether this problem of the successful shaping of musical form was not connected in some way with the strange fact that musical history names no women in its

43

roster of great composers. There have been great women musical interpreters, but thus far — I emphasize, *thus far* — no examples of women composers of the first rank. This is a touchy subject, no doubt, but leaving aside the obscure and various reasons for the historical fact, it appears to indicate that the conception and shaping of abstract ideas in extended forms marks a clear boundary between the creative mind and the interpretative mind.

In all that I have been saying about creative thinking there is implied the strongly imaginative quality of the artist's mentality. I stress this now because there has been a tendency in recent times to put the emphasis rather on the artist as craftsman, with much talk of the composer's technique. The artist-craftsman of the past is held up to us as the model to be emulated. There is a possible source of confusion here: amidst all the talk of the craftsmanlike approach we must always remember that a work of art is not a pair of shoes. It may very well be useful like a pair of shoes, but it takes its source from a quite different sphere of mental activity. Roger Sessions understood this when he wrote recently: "The composer's technique is, on the lowest level, his mastery of the musical language . . . On a somewhat higher level . . . it becomes identical with his musical thought, and it is problematical in terms of substance rather than merely of execution. On this level it is no longer accurate to speak of craftsmanship. The composer is no longer simply a craftsman; he has become a musical thinker, a creator of values — values which are primarily aesthetic, hence psychological, but hence, as an inevitable consequence, ultimately of the deepest human importance."

It is curious that this concern with craftsmanship should have affected an art that has developed no successful large-scale primitive practitioners, in the sense that there are accepted primitive painters. Music boasts no Henri Rousseau, no Grandma Moses. Naiveté doesn't work in music. To write any sort of a usable piece presumes a minimum kind of professionalism. Mussorgsky and Satie are the

44

closest we have come in recent times to a primitive composer, and the mere mention of their names makes the idea rather absurd.

No, I suspect that the stress placed upon the composer as craftsman, especially in teacher-pupil relationships, comes from a basic mistrust of making private aesthetic judgments. There is the fear of being wrong, plus the insecurity of not being able to *prove* that one is right, even to oneself. As a result an attitude is encouraged of avoiding the whole messy business of aesthetic evaluation, putting one's attention on workmanship and craft instead, for there we deal in solid values. But that attitude, to my mind, side-steps the whole question of the composer's own need for critical awareness and for making aesthetic judgments at the moment of creation. As I see it, this ability is part of his craft, and the lack of it has weakened, when it hasn't entirely eliminated, many potentially fine works.

The creative mind, in its day-to-day functioning, must be a critical mind. The ideal would be not merely to be aware, but to be "aware of our awareness," as Professor I. A. Richards has put it. In music this self-critical appraisal of the composer's own mind guiding the composition to its inevitable termination is particularly difficult of application, for music is an emotional and comparatively intangible substance. Composers, especially young composers, are not always clear as to the role criticism plays at the instant of creation. They don't seem to be fully aware that each time one note is followed by another note, or one chord by another chord, a decision has been made. They seem even less aware of the psychological and emotional connotations of their music. Instead they appear to be mainly concerned with the purely formal rightness of a general scheme, with a particular care for the note-for-note logic of thematic relationships. In other words, they are partially aware, but not fully aware, and not sufficiently cognizant of those factors which have a controlling influence on the success or failure of the composition as a whole. A full and equal appraisal of every smallest contributing

45

factor, with an understanding of the controlling and most essential elements in the piece, without allowing this to cramp one's freedom of creative inventiveness — being, as it were, inside and outside the work at the same time; that is how I envisage the "awareness of one's awareness." Beethoven's genius was once attributed by Schubert to what he termed his "superb coolness under the fire of creative fantasy." What a wonderful way to describe the creative mind functioning at its highest potential!

It is one of the curiosities of the critical creative mind that although it is very much alive to the component parts of the finished work, it cannot know everything that the work may mean to others. There is an unconscious part in each work — an element that André Gide called *la part de Dieu*. I have often felt familiar, and yet again unfamiliar, with a new work of mine as it was being rehearsed for the first time — as if both the players and I myself had to accustom ourselves to its strangeness. The late Paul Rosenfeld once wrote that he saw the steel frames of skyscrapers in my Piano Variations. I like to think that the characterization was apt, but I must confess that the notion of skyscrapers was not at all in my mind when I was composing the Variations. In similar fashion an English critic, Wilfrid Mellers, has found in the final movement of my Piano Sonata "a quintessential musical expression of the idea of immobility." "The music runs down like a clock," Mellers writes, "and dissolves away into eternity." That is probably a very apt description also, although I would hardly have thought of it myself. Composers often tell you that they don't read criticisms of their works. As you see, I am an exception. I admit to a curiosity about the slightest cue as to the meaning of a piece of mine — a meaning, that is, other than the one I know I have put there.

Quite apart from my own curiosity, there is always the question of how successfully one is communicating with an audience. A composer who cannot in advance calculate to some extent the effect of his piece on the listening public is in for some rude awakenings.

46

Whether or not he ought to take this effect upon an audience into account at the time of composing is another matter. Here again composers vary widely in their attitude. But whatever they tell you, I think it is safe to assume that although a conscious desire for communication may not be in the forefront of their minds, every move toward logic and coherence in composing is in fact a move toward communication. It is only a slight step when a composer tries for coherence in terms of a particular audience. This idea of music directed to a particular public is usually a bit shocking to the music-lover. It doesn't matter how many times we tell the familiar story of Bach writing each week for the honest burghers of Leipzig, or Mozart's relations with the courtly musical patrons of his day; audiences still prefer to think of the musical creator as a man closeted with his idea, unsullied by the rough and tumble of the world around him. Whether or not contemporary composers think about this matter of communication with their audience, they haven't been signally successful at it. The reasons for this are explored in greater detail in a later chapter.

The subject of communication with an audience brings us quite naturally to a consideration of the performer's role, and the inter-action of the creative and the interpretative mind which is crucial to the whole musical experience. These two functions — creation and interpretation — were usually performed, in pre-Beethoven days, by a single individual. The composer was his own interpreter; or, as frequently happened, interpreters wrote music for their own in-strument. But nowadays, as we all know, these functions are more usually separated, and the composer is in the position of a man who has lost his power of speech and consigns his thoughts by letter to an audience that cannot read words. Consequently they both have need of a middleman, a talented reader who can arouse response in an audience by the public reading of the composer's message.

A prime question immediately presents itself: what does the com-poser expect of his reader, or interpreter? I think I know what one

of the main preoccupations of the interpreter is: elocutionary eloquence, or, to put it in musical terms, the making of beautiful
sounds. All his life long he has trained himself to overcome all
technical hurdles and to produce the most admirable tone obtainable
on his instrument. But there's the rub; the composer is thinking
about something quite different. He is concerned not so much with
technical adequacy or quality of tonal perfection as with the character and specific expressive nature of the interpretation. Whatever
else happens he doesn't want his basic conception to be falsified. At
any moment he is ready to sacrifice beauty of tone for the sake of a
more meaningful reading. Every performing artist has something
of the elocutionist in him; he wants the words to shine, and the
sound of them to be full and right. Every composer, on the other
hand, has something of a playwright in him; he wants above all to
have his "actors" intent upon the significance of a scene, on its import within a particular context, for if that is lost, all elocutionary
eloquence becomes meaningless — irritating even, since it hinders
the creative mind from getting across to the auditor the whole point
and purpose of the work of art.

Further analogies with playacting exist. The notion of the actress
who has been hopelessly miscast in a play is familiar to all of us.
But musical actors, so to speak, often miscast themselves, and with
less justification. The woman violinist who has the robust, healthy
tone of a washerwoman will never successfully invoke from her
instrument the sweet innocence of a *jeune fille*. The singer who is a
nice person, and who possesses an excellent voice, may have no
inner comprehension for the tragic sense of life, and hence will
never successfully communicate that sentiment. One might almost
maintain that musical interpretation demands of the performer an
even wider range than that of the actor, because the musician must
play every role in the piece.

At this point I can hear the querulous performer asking: But is
there only *one* way of reading a piece of music? Aren't divergent

readings of the same music possible? Most certainly they are. As a composer I should like to think that any one of my works is capable of being read in several ways. Otherwise a work might be said to lack richness of meaning. But each different reading must in itself be convincing, musically and psychologically — it must be within the limits of one of the possible ways of interpreting the work. It must have stylistic truth, which is to say it must be read within the frame of reference that is true for the composer's period and individual personality.

This question of the proper style in playing or singing is one of the thornier problems of music. There have been instances when I have listened to performances of my work and thought: this is all very fine, but I don't think I recognize myself. It may be that the performer misses the folklike simplicity I had intended, or that he underplays the monumental tone at the conclusion of a piece, or that he overemphasizes the grotesque element in a scherzo section. Personally I have always found the finest interpreters most ready to accept a composer's suggestions. And similarly, it is from the finest interpreters that the composer can learn most about the character of his work; aspects of it that he did not realize were there, tempi that are slower or faster than he had himself imagined were the correct ones, phrasings that better express the natural curve of a melody. Here is where the interaction of composer and interpreter can be most fruitful.

All questions of interpretation sooner or later resolve themselves into a discussion of how faithful the performer ought to be to the notes themselves. No sooner do we ask this than a counterquestion suggests itself: how faithful are composers to the notes they themselves put down? Some performers take an almost religious attitude to the printed page: every comma, every slurred staccato, every metronomic marking is taken as sacrosanct. I always hesitate, at least inwardly, before breaking down that fond illusion. I wish our notation and our indications of tempi and dynamics were that exact, but honesty compels me to admit that the written page is only an approximation; it's only an indication of how close the composer was able to come in transcribing his exact thoughts on paper. Beyond that point the interpreter is on his own. I know that there are some contemporary composers who have been exasperated by the extreme liberties taken with the notes by romantic artists. As a result they have gone to the other extreme and said: "Stop concerning yourselves with interpretation, just play the notes." That attitude blithely ignores the insufficiencies of musical notation, and thus refuses to take into account the realities of the situation. The only sensible advice one can give a performing artist is to ask that a happy balance be found between slavish adherence to inadequate signs and a too liberal straying from the clear intentions of the composer.

In order to get insight into the interpreter's mentality it is necessary to be able to bring judgment to bear on the performance. The interpretation itself must be interpreted if we are to evaluate what the executant is contributing to a performance. This is not easy for the layman. Observation has convinced me that even the truly musical layman often has difficulty in making subtle distinctions in the judging of musical performance. He seems to lack the criteria necessary for such critical judgment. The difficulty arises from the fact that the listener, in order to exercise such criteria, is expected to know in advance what the performance *ought* to sound like before he hears what it *does* sound like. In other words, he must have an ideal performance in his mind's ear alongside which he can place the actual performance heard for purposes of comparison. To do this he must understand, first, the style appropriate to the historical period of the composition and to the composer's development up to that time; and secondly, he must be able to describe precisely the nature of the given execution so that he can particularize the qualities special to that performer and none other. To do this well presupposes wide historical knowledge, a great deal of experience in listening, with the admixture of an instinctive musicality of one's own.

In interpreting the interpretation, as I put it, we must never lose sight of the preponderant role of the individual personality of the performer. I like to think that if I were to hear successively three unidentified pianists behind a screen I could give you a brief personality sketch of each one of them, and come somewhere near the truth. This may of course be merely an illusion of mine, but no matter; it indicates what I mean by the thought that a performance is both an exposition of the piece and an exposition of the personality traits of the performer. This is particularly true for singers. Like actors on the stage, they must be impressive in themselves, even before they utter a sound. Singers are really "on the spot"; unlike the conductor they cannot turn their backs to us; they face us, and the song and the personality are inextricably mixed. You can't get at the one except through the other. The same is true of instrumentalists, except that in their case our sight of the instrument and their busy fingers makes less obvious the role played by personality. But it is there nonetheless. When a performer lacks personality we call the performance dull; when he has too much personality we complain that he obscures the piece from view. A just appreciation of the exact part played by the performer's personality in any given execution is therefore essential for precise judgment.

Now let us get down to cases. Let us observe the interpreter in action, for the purpose of describing certain basic psychological types that are met with most frequently.

Great interpretation, as the "big" public understands it, is generally of the fiery and romantic type. Since so much of the music we hear publicly performed comes from the romantic period, many performers are forced to adopt the manner, even though they may not be born to it. But the true romantic — the interpreter who creates an impression of giving himself in an uninhibited way — has great power over audiences everywhere. I am now thinking in terms of the real thing, not merely of the unfortunate individual making a public spectacle of himself. By only a slim margin a tasteless exhibitionism is separated from an experience that can be deeply moving. When this kind of performance doesn't come off, we want to laugh — if we are charitably inclined; in less charitable moments it can be infuriating, for the simulation of strong feelings on the part of an interpreter who is really feeling nothing at all strikes us as a public lie; we want to rise up and denounce it. On the other hand, the performer who is deeply moved, and who without a shadow of embarrassment can openly appeal to what is warmest and most human in man's psyche, and who in a sense exhibits himself in this state of vibrant sympathy before the glazed stare of a large and heterogeneous crowd — that is the performer who really communicates with an audience and who usually wins the loudest plaudits.

Another of the truly potent ways of engendering legitimate excitement in an audience is for the player or singer to give the impression that chances are being taken. To create this kind of excitement there must really be a precarious element present. There must be danger: danger that the performance will get out of hand; that the performer, no matter how phenomenal his natural gift may be, has set himself a task that is possibly beyond even his capability of realizing it.

Nothing is so boring as a merely well-rehearsed performance, well-rehearsed in the sense that nothing can be expected to happen except what was studiously prepared in advance. This has vitiated more than one tasteful and careful performance. It is as if the musician, during the execution, had stopped listening to himself, and was simply performing a duty rather than a piece. It is axiomatic that unless the hearing of the music first stirs the executant it is unlikely to move an audience. A live performance should be just that — live to all the incidents that happen along the way, colored

52

by the subtle nuances of momentary emotion, inspired by the sudden insights of public communication. Wonderful performances can be of many different kinds, but the virtuoso performance that is breathlessly exciting, to my mind, always implies this almost-but-not-quite out-of-control quality, the antithesis of the well-rehearsed execution.

Still another type of performer, whose sphere of action is somewhere in the neighborhood of the romantic, is the musician who gives a personalized reading of a work. Every performance that has been logically conceived represents a reading in some sense, but in this case the reading is more particularized and personalized, so that the composition is not just the composition, but the composition as our performer on that one occasion understands its meaning and tries to communicate it. In the case of a conductor of this type, thoughts of elegance of style, perfection of ensemble, delicacy of instrumental balance are all secondary; instead he is "singing" his way through the composition with a kind of concentration that does not allow for distractions of mere technical details. Such a reading, to be successful, must impose itself — must break down the resistance that may come from the thought that you or I might read the work differently. There can be no question of "aesthetic contemplation" here, either for the conductor or his listener. What he strives for is our involvement in a wholeness of experience — the sense that he and his listeners have lived through something important. This is the kind of performer who sometimes takes a meretricious piece and makes it sound better than it really is. The power of conviction behind such a performance tends to blot out critical reservations. We lend ourselves, and smile about it later. It was a good show, we got our money's worth, and no one was really fooled. But when the work merits it, and the reading is truly convincing, we are left with the impression that whether or not what we have heard is the only possible interpretation, we have at least heard *one* of the essential ways in which that music is to be understood.

I should like to invoke now another category of performer whose mind seems concentrated on a quite different artistic end; the performer whose approach to interpretation is more impersonal, more classic perhaps. Here the objective is an absolute clarity of texture, a euphonious ensemble, an infallible sense of timing, and above all, prime concern with continuity and flow — the sense of directional movement forward which is intrinsic to the nature and character of all music. Here it is not the musical measure being heard that is important but the musical measure to come. It is this concern with forward motion that carries a piece in one long trajectory from its beginning to its end and gives an interpretation inevitability.

The interpreter whose attention is focused on the road ahead is better able than others to give us the long line and sculptural shape of a composition. It is useless to explain this need for directional movement forward to performers who have no instinct for it. They may, and often do have clarity, but clarity taken by itself can easily decline in interest to that of a schoolroom demonstration — a laboratory taking-apart of the mechanics of a piece of music. We see how it ticks in its minutest part. For some reason, however, unless an inner fervor is generated, the performer becomes a schoolmaster who makes the composition clear for us but neglects somehow to turn it into music.

There is another attribute of the classic approach to the re-creation of music that should be mentioned: the species of deep satisfaction to be derived from a performance that has ease and relaxation. Effortless singing or playing is one of the major joys of music listening: it indicates a measure of mental confidence and a degree of physical assurance in the handling of the instrument, whatever it may be, that is not often found in combination in one human being. There are few qualities more grateful in execution than this sense of ease, the sense of powers completely adequate to the expressive purpose, but few things are more difficult to achieve for the per-

54

former. This is not at all a matter of the intellect, for certain performers in the field of popular music also have this kind of ease — in fact, they are more likely to possess it than are concert artists. I doubt whether it can be tricked. It must reflect a true inner relaxation, difficult to come by in view of the condition of public performance, which in itself makes for tension. But the master interpreters have it.

I have left until last the question of national characteristics in musical interpretation. Is there such a thing? Is there an American way of performing Schubert as distinguished from an Austrian way? It seems to me that there most definitely is. The quickest way of gauging this is to compare present-day American and European orchestral performance. Our orchestras, by comparison with those abroad, are energized and glamorized: they play with a golden sheen that reflects their material well-being. The European organization approaches orchestral performance in a more straightforward and natural way. There is less sense of strain, less need to make each execution the "world's greatest." In Europe it gives one a feeling of refreshment to come upon the frankly unglamorous playing of a solidly trained orchestra. I once heard such an orchestra in America, about fifteen years ago. It came out of the Middle West and played under a conductor of European origin in such a way that one felt the whole organization had just stepped out of the nineteenth century. Nowadays, when that approach is attempted, it generally results in a businesslike, shipshape rendition, without much artistic conviction behind it. More typical is the glorified tonal approach, although our orchestras still have not reached the steely brass perfection of a jazz combination's attack. But something of the same compulsion to "wow" an audience through the sheer power of tonal magnificence is present. Our symphonic organizations, as they become known in Europe, are admired for their live sound and their vitality in performance. It is only right that they should be. My

55

object is not to belittle the outstanding qualities of our orchestras but merely to stress one factor in their playing which seems to me indicative of national flavor.

National characteristics are most clearly present in interpretation, I suppose, when it can be said that the execution is "in the true tradition." This comes about when the performer is either a contemporary of the composer and has received the correct style of rendition through association with the composer himself, or when, by birth and background, the performer is identified in our minds with the country and culture — sometimes even the city — of the composer in question. I realize that the phrase "in the true tradition" is at best a shaky one. For there is no positive proof that my conception of the "true tradition" is the really true one. Still, we are all mostly ready to concede that the conductor from Vienna has a special insight into the way in which Schubert should be played. Serge Koussevitzky once made an observation to me that I shall always remember. He said that our audiences would never entirely understand American orchestral compositions until they heard them conducted by American-born conductors. It seems clear, then, that if we can speak of national traits of character, inevitably those traits will form the interpreter's character as a human being and shine through the interpretation.

In sketching thus briefly various basic types of interpreter I have naturally been forced to oversimplification. The finest artists cannot be so neatly pigeonholed, as I am afraid I may have suggested. The reason we remain so alive to their qualities is just because in each case we are forced to balance and adjust subtle gradations of interpretative power. Every new artist, and for that matter every new composer, is a problem child — a composite of virtues and defects that challenges the keenness of mind of the listener.

I have mentioned what the composer expects from his interpreter. I should now logically state what the interpreter expects from the composer. Too often, however, the truth is that interpreters are not thinking about the composer at all — I mean the live composer. In the past it was different. There are numerous instances of a work being written simply because some outstanding instrumentalist inspired it. Paganini commissioning Berlioz, Joachim helping Brahms — instances such as these become more legendary as the years pass. Of course isolated examples still occur, but for the most part a regrettable gulf separates the interpreter and composer in present-day musical life. They are not interacting enough! A healthy musical state of affairs would include increased opportunities for interpreters and composers to meet and exchange ideas. This should begin at the school level, as often happened abroad. If I were an interpreter I think I should like to have the sense that I had been a part of the full musical experience of my time, which inevitably means an active part in the development of the composers of my time. Is this too utopian? I hope not, because the indissoluble link between interpreter and composer makes their interaction one of the conditions of a healthily functioning musical community.

Part Two

MUSICAL IMAGINATION IN THE CONTEMPORARY SCENE

CHAPTER FOUR

Tradition and Innovation in Recent European Music

"MUSIC, MORE THAN ANY OTHER ART, is born under the law of tradition." That sentence, from an article by the French critic, Frederick Goldbeck, occurred to me as I was being shown about the venerable palazzo that houses the Benedetto Marcello musical conservatory in Venice. "The composer's chords," Goldbeck had written, "are every dead or living composer's chords, never his own. His paper is never a blank; there are so many staves on it, five prison bars in each, History and Tradition being the jail . . ." These phrases echoed in my mind as the conservatory's director, Francesco Malipiero, led me down the ancient corridors and dusted off for me to examine precious musical manuscripts inherited from other centuries. Suddenly it struck me, in a way it never had before, to what an extent the European musician is forced into the position of acting as caretaker and preserver of other men's music, whether he likes it or no. Malipiero himself, at that moment, seemed to symbolize the essential dilemma of the European musician, for he has been both the editor of Monteverdi's complete works and, at the same time, one of the leading composers in Italy's twentieth-century musical renaissance.

The pull of tradition as against the attraction of innovation are the two polar forces that constitute the basic drama of today's European music. Not so long ago, especially under the impact of the neo-classic movement in contemporary music, the impression gained currency that the "revolutionary" era in music was over, and that the turmoil created by the extensions in harmonic language and the change in aesthetic ideals had gradually subsided, leaving us with a musical idiom that held no surprises for any of us. But is this still a true picture of the state of affairs at present? Or is it now time to reëxamine the situation? It seems to me that once again the European composer is writing his music under the sign of crisis; and in order to examine the nature of that crisis it will be necessary to look closely at those trends in contemporary music that stress traditional values and those that constitute a threat to such values.

It is quite evident that there is no further revolution possible in the harmonic sphere, none, at any rate, so long as we confine ourselves to the tempered scale and its normal division by half tones. There is no such thing any longer as an inadmissible chord, or melody, or rhythm — given the proper context, of course. Contemporary practice has firmly established that fact. As I see it, the "threat" to tradition, if it is a "threat," lies elsewhere, and is of two kinds.

The first has to do with the assumptions that underlie our ideas concerning the structure and organization of musical coherence. Arnold Schönberg was the composer whose work produced the crisis in that sphere. The second has to do with the social import and basic purpose of musical creation today, and it is a question which continues to hound us all. It was given formal declaration by the publication of a manifesto signed by a group of composers from various countries meeting in Prague in 1948. Both these problems are foremost in the minds of many of Europe's best musical creators today.

I shall launch boldly into a consideration of the breakdown in the formal organization of music, in an attempt to find out how such a breakdown came about and, if possible, what it's implications may be.

Music is, by nature, the most amorphous of the arts; it is continually in danger of falling apart. The story of composition might be told in terms of the devices employed, always tentatively at first, and then finally in full flower, which produced formal patterns that give some semblance of cohesion to music. The forms of one age are not necessarily those of another, the surprising thing being that they last as long as they do. At the present time we are the inheritors of a good many set forms — the chaconne, the fugue, the sonata, to name a few — which have served composers for some two hundred years or more. These and other forms provide the composer with an outward mould into which he may pour his ideas with some assurance that they will coalesce and make sense to the listener. I hasten to add, however, that composers have a special relationship to the set form which is not always clear to the layman. A composer does not simply "pack his materials" into "pre-existing moulds." A set form is nothing more than a "generalization," as Donald Tovey calls it. As he points out, we must generalize from a detailed experience of the behavior of individual works, and must not try to explain that behavior by the generalization. In other words, each separate composition is a law unto itself, and only bears a general resemblance to the external shape of whatever form is adopted. This explains, in large measure, the reason for the longevity of these forms. It also explains why textbooks on structure in music are of only limited usefulness to the music student. For the more closely he adheres to their abstract form-types the further he will be from the truly creative act, which gives to the particular material at hand the shape and cohesion that only it may have.

The question then suggests itself: to what extent are these set forms a necessity? Without them would music be chaotic? Or are certain time-honored forms a hindrance rather than a help, and is it merely a sentimental attachment on the part of composers that keeps them alive? In this connection, the report of a conversation that Ferruccio Busoni is said to have had with a pupil of his in 1922 is pertinent. Busoni, by the time he was a mature musician, had completely lost patience with the conventionality of "official" German music, the *Kapellmeistermusik* of the end of the nineteenth century. In 1907 he published a slim volume in which he envisaged a day when music would be free, that is, free of any formal plan that might be characterized as "architectonic," or "symmetric," or "sectional." "Music," he said, "was born free; and to win freedom is its destiny." He thought that composers had come closest to uncovering the true nature of music in "preparatory and intermediary passages (preludes and transitions) where they felt at liberty to disregard symmetrical proportions and unconsciously drew free breath." In 1922 he was still laboring the point, and this time the fugue was his target. This is how he put it: "The fugue is a form, and as such is bound to its time. It was Bach who found its principle and its essential realization. Today, also, one can write fugues, and I would even recommend it; one can even compose them with the most contemporary means . . . But even in such a form, the fugue is no less archaic; it always has the effect of archaizing the music, and it cannot pretend to give it its expression and its actual meaning."

What are we to conclude? Have fugues and other old forms become hopelessly old-fashioned? Are they so many strait jackets which have finally outlived their usefulness? Whether we answer yes or no, it seems to me that as long as basically tonal music is written certain fundamental controlling factors will be present. Roger Sessions once summarized these as: first, the sense of progression or cumulation; second, the association for repetition of ideas; third, the feeling for contrast. Given these requisites, a piece of music may be constructed without reference to any established set form and yet have a tight, precise, and logical shape. In any essentially tonal piece this would be accomplished through the rational progression of the underlying harmonies, through the relationships of melodies or melodic fragments, through rhythmic unity, and through a general sense of dramatic and psychological truth.

My point is that the working out of these requirements will produce a composition whose governing principles will be the same, in essence, whether or not the design is free or well known. It is precisely this possibility of endless variety in applying basic principles of formal coherence that has made it possible for composers in the past, and seems likely to make it possible for them in the future, to continue the writing of passacaglia, scherzo, theme and variations, and so forth without fear of exhausting the value of the generalized mould.

This tendency toward the conservation of old forms and their reinterpretation in modern terms is representative of the pull toward tradition in Europe's music. It was accentuated by the return to eighteenth-century ideals that characterized the neoclassical movement in the middle twenties. Neoclassicism, at the time Stravinsky originated it, acted as a brake on the chaotic postwar period. It also served as an antidote to the vaguenesses of impressionism, for it is interesting to note that some of the composers most intrigued by neoclassic forms — Alfredo Casella, Manuel de Falla, Albert Roussel — had all previously written music in the post-Debussy manner. Sooner than anyone thought possible, the Russian whose name had been a symbol of upheaval in music became the stimulus for a more conservative attitude. But, as always, Stravinsky himself knew how to remain vitally alive within the confines of any self-imposed restriction. By now, the neoclassic tendency, insofar as it exists as a general movement in present-day music, appears to be definitely on the wane. It seems to have run its natural course and exhausted its usefulness. The classicalizing principles involved retain their validity, no doubt, but the specific references to eighteenth-century mannerisms and turns of phrase have lost whatever interest they once had.

The composer who has been most outspoken and most consistent in his attitude toward the conservation of firmly grounded principles is, of course, Paul Hindemith. As a young man he was beguiled by several of the shibboleths of the twenties, but by the time he was thirty-five he had reacted violently. His writings have made perfectly clear the doctrines that he applies to his own compositions; and in his finest pieces it is a marvel to behold these same doctrines filled out with inspired music. The Hindemithian theories will always have most appeal to those minds that feel comfortable only with a closely reasoned and systematic approach to any problem. My own mind feels more at home with the unsystematic approach of writers like Montaigne and Goethe, let us say; and especially in the field of music it seems to me important that we keep open what William James calls the "irrational doorways . . . through which . . . the wildness and the pang of life" may be glimpsed. The systematic and the irrational are mutually exclusive; and that is why Hindemith's tenets, clarified and truthful as far as they go, are inherently limited and cannot hope to encompass the oftentimes instinctual drives of the creative mechanism.

It is to England that one must turn in order to find a whole school of significant composers who put their faith in tradition. It isn't that England has no dodecaphonic composers, but the men who have made the strongest impression — Ralph Vaughan Williams, William Walton, Benjamin Britten, Michael Tippett — are all solid musical citizens, upholders of traditional values. Despite this conformist outlook, each one of them has his individual musical style. All are, in greater or less degree, masters of the rhetorical musical gesture, especially Britten, the youngest among them. His music, and especially his operas, are an excellent example of how, by working within clearly planned forms and by having a brilliant technical equipment for the carrying out of any possible plan, one can achieve breadth, variety, richness with a familiar idiom. This greatly gifted Britisher, not yet forty, has every known compositional resource at his command, which perhaps explains his unconcerned acceptance of traditional methods and ideals. His work, diatonic and stylized as it is, has placed English music, after a hiatus of more than two

66

hundred years, in the mainstream of present-day European musical history.

Michael Tippett is another member of the new generation of British composers with strong sympathy for the traditional approach. Tippett, unlike Britten whose models are drawn from more eclectic sources, has been attracted by certain procedures of the Elizabethan composers of the late sixteenth century. Tippett himself describes the opening movement of his Second String Quartet as "partly derived from madrigal technique where each part may have its own rhythm and the music is propelled by the differing accents, which tend to thrust each other forward." This fondness for cross-rhythms gives his music at times a certain relationship to American music. (There are certain melodic sections in Vaughan Williams' Sixth Symphony which seem to me strikingly American also.) Tippett lacks the sureness of touch that characterizes the music of Britten or Walton, but his music exemplifies better than theirs the attempt to contain within conservative limits a naturally effusive temperament. In Sir William Walton we have a child of the hectic twenties who has been turned into a pillar of British musical society. All adventuresomeness has completely gone out of his work. We are left with "solid values," but with little else. (I refer to the recent works.) In Walton's case we must go back to the Viola Concerto of the late twenties in order to find an excellent example of the rethinking in contemporary language of familiar techniques in composition.

The roster of traditionally-minded composers might be greatly extended — Honegger in France, Petrassi in Italy, Boris Blacher in Germany — because the between-the-wars period was mainly one of consolidating the gains of the preceding quarter of a century of unrest. Shortly after the end of the last war, however, it became clear that a considerable number of composers in various countries had begun to write a music that constituted a threat to this newly gained stability, and especially threatened the structural organization of music as it had been formerly understood. It is interesting to remember that in its origination this threat came from exactly that quarter where one would least expect it: Vienna, the fount of classical traditions; and from one man, Arnold Schönberg, who, ironically enough, professed a passionate regard for these same classics. Schönberg used to refer to himself as a victim, as a man who had reluctantly taken upon himself the Promethean role of destroying the tonal system, a system which had required hundreds of years to develop. It was serious enough to have undermined the tonal system, for in so doing, Schönberg condemned himself to writing a music that was certain to sound, so to speak, "wrong" to its first listeners. But the man who undermined tonal harmony, was *ipso facto* undermining the fundamental structure of musical form, for that also is premised on the ordered progression of related tonalities. Schönberg was fully aware of the enormity of his act, as is proved by the fact that for a long time he composed nothing in the larger forms (his first post-tonal pieces had all been short), after which there followed a silence that lasted for eight years.

Schönberg was not a man hankering after freedom, like Busoni. Far from it; he was seeking a new discipline to substitute for the one he had made obsolete by the abandonment of tonality. After the long silence, during which time he was occupied with tentative probings toward a solution of his problem, he emerged with a new *modus operandi,* the "method of composing with the twelve tones," as he preferred to name it. As finally perfected by Schönberg, the method guaranteed the control of every tone in the musical fabric, since, melodically and harmonically, it was based on a perpetual use through variation of a chosen arrangement or series of the twelve chromatic tones. Note well that his premise was not a melody; it was an arrangement of tones that could be manipulated in a great number of ways, and yet had the added advantage of being under rigorous control at every instant. Even the most radical step, it appears, must be accompanied, in the mind of the German-trained musician, by logic and control.

There is no doubt that Schönberg and his followers derived great stimulus from this new method. Without the evidence of the music itself one might imagine that all ties with tonal music had been broken. But strangely enough, the classicist in Schönberg was not to be so easily downed, and so we find him writing string quartets in the customary four movements, each separate movement partaking somewhat of the usual expressive content, and the general outlines recognizably those of a first-movement allegro, a minuet, a slow movement, and a rondo. Alban Berg, even before his adoption of the twelve-tone method, had written his opera *Wozzeck* in such a way that each of the fifteen scenes is based on some normal set form — a passacaglia, a military march, a series of inventions, and so forth. Anton Webern, in many of his works, wrote canons and variations. Other twelve-tone composers followed suit. An extraordinarily paradoxical situation developed: despite the rigorous organization of the twelve tones according to the dictates of the series and its mutations, and despite the adoption at times of the outward semblance of traditional shapes, the effect the music makes in actual performance is often one of near-chaos.

We are faced, then, with two seemingly opposite facts: on the one hand the music is carefully plotted in its every detail; and on the other it undeniably creates an anarchic impression. On the one hand the musical journals of every country are filled with articles explaining the note-for-note logic of Schönbergian music, accompanied by appropriate graphs, abstracts, and schematized reductions, enormous ingenuity being expended on the tracking down of every last refinement in an unbelievably complex texture. (One gains the impression that it is not the music before which the commentators are lost in admiration so much as the way in which it lends itself to detailed analysis.) But on the other hand, when we return to the concert hall and listen once again to these same compositions we leave with the disturbing memory of a music that borders on chaos.

What are we to conclude? Quite simply that these innovators are more revolutionary than they themselves know or are willing to admit. While appearing to have engineered merely a harmonic revolution, and set up a new method of composing in its place, they have in actuality done away with all previous conceptions of the normal flow of music.

I regret having taken so long to arrive at a point that the reader might have been willing to concede at the outset. But it is important to my argument to establish the fact itself — the loss of the normal flow of music — because of the implications it carries with it.

These implications are most clearly discernible in the music of Schönberg's pupil Anton Webern. More and more the postwar twelve-tone developments point to Webern as the key man in the situation — the man who carried Schönberg's ideas to their furthest limits. The music that Webern himself wrote, and the influence it has exerted on younger minds is possibly the most singular phenomenon of our times. It is a singular experience also to attempt to read Webern's music at the piano. It has a curious way of rebuffing you; it — so to speak — *defies* you to read it. It has a disconcerting look on the page: it seems wayward and unpredictable, with a minimum number of notes and a maximum number of rests between the notes. On the face of it the music seems arbitrary and planless, but as a matter of demonstrable fact, it can be shown that this is the most implacably controlled music Europe has ever known. The look of it may be incoherent, but the sound of it I think is fascinating, although the music's scope and breadth of expression are matters that have not yet been fully tested.

Putting aside the question of expression, there are two features in Webern's music which in effect circumvent all tonal practice and suggest unexplored possibilities for the future. First, there is the matter of melody. When modern music was a term to frighten people with, an often-heard reproach used to be: the stuff lacks melody. Carefully, we used to explain that it was simply a question of extending one's idea of what a melody might be, and in that case, assuming you could unravel it from the unfamiliar harmonic texture, it would be found that modern music had as much melodic content as older music. But in Webern's work the composer starts not with a theme, but with a predetermined arrangement of the twelve tones of the chromatic scale, from which an immense number of *possible* melodies might be subsumed. The thing to remember is that although each melody or melodic fragment relates back to the skeletal series, no one of them need bear any recognizable relation to any other, at least so far as the ear is concerned. As a result no one melody is given predominance; therefore there are no themes as such, and all possibility of even a single repetition of a theme is canceled out. (For purposes of simplification I am ignoring the literal repetition of entire sections.) We are faced therefore with a music which is at every instant new. Thus, the old familiar landmarks of "normal" music are gone — such as thematic relationships and developments — and the phrase "to recognize a theme" becomes absolutely meaningless. We have arrived at a musical art which is constructed on unfamiliar principles: the world of athematic music.

A second field in which Webern's music has had unusual suggestive value is that of rhythm. This, the most primitive element in music, has always remained comparatively free of constraint. Rhythm was considered to need no justification; it was judged by its naturalness of movement and limited by no laws other than those of unity and variety. A close examination of Webern's later music will show that his passion for logic and control applies also to the rhythmic factor, for it follows that when melodic phrases are subjected to strict manipulation and an almost continual canonic treatment, inevitably the underlying rhythmic structure will be under strict control also. In Webern's last works one gets the impression that no single instant of the rhythmic play is left to chance, so that it becomes possible to envisage a music whose sole structural principle will be that of rhythmic control. Webern's rhythms produce an effect of calculated discontinuity that has no precedent in other men's music.

New interest in purely rhythmic experimentation must have been in the air, for we find a similar attitude expounded in the theoretical works and exemplified in the music of the French composer Olivier Messiaen. This Catholic organist-composer has freely acknowledged his debt to a variety of sources, and especially to the rhythmic flexibilities of Hindu *rāgas* and *tālas* as a source of rhythmic inspiration. Messiaen's researches led him to subject rhythms to the same type of contrapuntal treatment that had usually been applied solely to melodic material, most of these familiar since Bach's day. Thus we get rhythmic canons, rhythmic organ points, or we may read a rhythm backwards as we used to revert a theme. Above all, in the imitation of rhythms in different parts, we may use not merely the usual augmentation or diminution of time values, but these may be inexactly imitated by the addition or subtraction of tiny metrical units, thereby guaranteeing an unusual rhythmic conformation.

These suggestive ideas were further developed by Messiaen's pupil, Pierre Boulez, who took as his point of departure the stylistic peculiarities of Webern and the rhythmic formulas of his teacher. The few Boulez scores that I have examined are of a truly formidable complexity. Questioned as to the necessity of so complex a texture, the composer maintained that, given the enormous variety of procedures open to the dodecaphonic composer, he was seeking for a corresponding "atonality" of the rhythmic frame. Boulez has a keen mind, an almost scientific one, I might say, and his investigations into new possibilities of formal organization through rhythmic control have already caused a considerable stir in *avant-garde* musical circles in Europe.

Boulez, for a certain time, came under the guidance of the French composer-critic René Leibowitz, the most indefatigable promulgator of the Schönbergian viewpoint in recent years. Leibowitz has had occasion, from time to time, to deplore the tendency of certain Schönberg followers to backslide: that is, to reintroduce basically tonal concepts into works that make use of the tone row in serial fashion. Schönberg himself, and certainly Alban Berg in his Violin Concerto, was guilty of injecting traces of tonality in an otherwise "pure" work. The man who is generally considered to be the leader in this more conservative wing of the dodecaphonic school is the Italian composer, Luigi Dallapiccola. There is no reason, Dallapiccola thinks, for limiting twelve-tone composers to the scholastic dictates of a Leibowitz. Now that the three pioneer leaders of the school have died it seems likely that new and unexpected derivations from the original system will appear. This possibility of freely applying the twelve-tone method, without necessarily accepting its atonal harmonic implications, seems to me to prove the power rather than the weakness of Schönberg's initial idea.

What, then, does all this add up to? Are we any nearer to the realization of Busoni's dream of a "free" music? "Creative power," Busoni wrote, "may be the more readily recognized, the more it shakes itself loose from tradition." By that touchstone the innovators in Europe have certainly succeeded in prying us loose from several age-old assumptions. That, it seems to me, is their prime importance. Whether we like or dislike any one example of their music or condemn their works *in toto,* the fact remains that they have put into question the basic assumptions on which were founded all former ideas about the flow and organization of European music. That in itself is no small achievement.

I began this chapter by saying that Europe's composers today are working under a sign of crisis. Now I wish to discuss the second part of that supposition: namely, the deep sense of concern about

73

the purpose and objective of composing today. Surprisingly, this subject is not as unrelated to twelve-tone composition and the problems it presents as might first appear.

Professor Edward Dent, who has for a good many years been an acute observer of the contemporary composer's activities, dates this phase of the "crisis" from Beethoven's day — the day when the creator of modern times was thrown back on his own resources, gaining indubitably in personal independence, but losing at the same time the assurance of an appointed place in society and the economic security that goes with it. This new independence left the composer uncertain for whom, exactly, he was writing his music. Professor Dent puts it this way: "The choice before the composer may appear to be a financial one, but that is negligible compared to the moral choice involved. Is he to write for himself only, to express his own individuality and then throw it in the face of the world with a 'take it or leave it,' or is he to regard his genius as something he holds in trust for the betterment of his fellow-creatures? That of course has always been the fundamental problem of all composers since Beethoven — the relation of the artist to the outside world." As I see it, there are really two questions involved here: first, that of the artist and his conscience — out of what inner conviction is he composing; and second, the artist and his communication — what musical language must he use in order to reach whatever audience he thinks may potentially be his?

These matters were, not so long ago, subjects for polite discussion. Nowadays they have taken on an air of grim reality. For the first time since Beethoven's day composers in certain countries are being told by those in a position of authority and with the ability to provide economic support exactly to whom their music ought to be directed, and in general terms what musical idiom and what forms best suit the purposes of communication. These recommendations were embodied in a declaration made by an international group of composers and musicologists meeting at Prague in 1948. It was the first time that composers from Great Britain, France, Holland, Switzerland, and other countries had allied themselves with composers from communist states in order to enunciate the so-called "progressive" point of view. If I read the declaration correctly, it simply states: we are entering a new era of human culture; therefore, works are wanted that are concrete in their message, particularly works that employ words — operas, oratorios, cantatas, songs, choruses, written in an understandable style using folk material, in order to counteract "cosmopolitan" tendencies. Dissonant contemporary music is out, or as they phrased it: "tendencies of extreme subjectivism" should be renounced.

All this is quite familiar by now, especially in view of the worldwide publicity afforded each fiat of Soviet musical policy. But the point is that from the perspective of the composer in noncommunist Europe it remains a vital issue. The lines are sharply drawn, and the battle is being fought out in the literary and musical journals of the various countries. The twelve-tone composer, especially, knows he is under fire; he is no longer writing music to satisfy himself; whether he likes it or not, he is writing it *against* a vocal and militant opposition. The composer of communist persuasion is no less concerned, for he has good reason to think that it may not be so easy to find the proper style that will appeal to the popular imagination and satisfy at the same time whatever artistic pretensions he himself may have. Thus, to put it flatly, the twelve-toners have a program, but little hope of reaching a popular audience; and the *progressivistes* have a potential audience, but no guarantee that they can invent a fresh musical manner appropriate to its needs. In between there are large numbers of practicing composers who live in a state of flux and semiconfusion, trying to avoid the brickbats from both parties. Circumstances, as never before, are forcing every serious European artist to face his conscience and attempt to find an answer to the questions of why and for whom his music is being written.

Every artist, whatever his convictions, must sooner or later face the problem of communication with an audience. The composer who is free to do as he pleases would do well to consider the advice of Professor I. A. Richards, penned some years ago. In substance he wrote that the artist need not consciously be aware of this problem, for even without knowing it he is deeply concerned with the matter of communication. If an artist occupies himself exclusively with getting a work "right" — "right" for himself, that is — it will communicate, because communication is part of its rightness. But, one must add, Professor Richards' artist enjoys the luxury of being right for himself alone; he is the free artist.

The artist who is not free has a great need for being consciously concerned with the matter of communication, for it is crucial to his situation. That situation has taken away from him one of the artist's most important rights, namely, the immemorial right of the artist to be wrong. A creator often learns as much from his miscalculations as he does from his successes. The need to be right every time must weigh heavily on the artist under communist supervision. My own guess is that the Soviet regime can hope for the kind of music they demand from their composers only if they develop a new species of artist who has never had any contact whatever with modern European music. For the artist who has once heard Milhaud or Hindemith, the apple of evil has been tasted and the "harm," from their standpoint, has been done. No composer who is even partially cognizant of our contemporary musical idiom will ever be able to fully eradicate its traces from his work. Therein lies the dilemma of the present-day Soviet composer, and especially of its leaders like Prokofieff and Shostakovich.

The musical situation as it exists abroad at the present time suggests no easy summary. In 1951 I spent six months in Europe, and when I think back and try to summarize my observations of the creative musical scene I must reluctantly admit that there are many disturbing factors in a situation that is anything but clarified. But how could it be otherwise? The only possible alternative would be for the composer to remove himself from all contact with the life about him, and that would be worse. No, we must expect Europe's music to reflect the many different tensions that characterize its political and spiritual life, for that is the only healthy way for it to exist. The surprising thing is not the variegated and rather confused picture that its many divisions create, but the fact that so much that is good and vital continues to be accomplished.

CHAPTER FIVE

Musical Imagination in the Americas

AN ASTUTE FELLOW MUSICIAN was responsible for suggesting to me the difficult subject of imagination in the music of the Americas. He put the question to me in this way: The art of music has been practiced for a good many years now in the Western Hemisphere — both north and south; can it be said that we have exercised our own imagination as musicians and not merely reflected what we have absorbed from Europe? And if we have succeeded in bringing a certain inventiveness and imaginativeness of our own to the world of music, what precisely has our contribution been? I protested that to answer such a question satisfactorily was an almost impossible assignment; that perhaps it was in any event too early to ask it; and, moreover, that I myself might be a poor judge of the present situation, because of an overanxiety to find favorable answers. But my musical friend persisted. He pointed out that everyone agrees that the two Americas are more grown-up musically than they were two generations ago; and besides, he added, you have visited South America and Mexico and Cuba and Canada, and have watched the musical movement in our own country develop for more than thirty years. Aren't you in a better position than most observers to arrive at some conclusion as to how far we have come in making our own special contribution to the world's music? In the end I found myself puzzling over this question. No matter how wrong-headed my reactions may be, it seemed likely that some musicologist fifty years hence might very well be intrigued to discover what answers suggested themselves to a composer in mid-twentieth century America.

If the experience of the Americas proves anything, it indicates that music is a sophisticated art — an art that develops slowly. It is about four hundred years since the first book containing musical notation was published in this hemisphere. That notable event took place in Mexico in the year 1556. In the United States the burgeoning period covers some three hundred years, which is also a considerable time span for the development of an art. Actually it seems to me that in order to create an indigenous music of universal significance three conditions are imperative. First, the composer must be part of a nation that has a profile of its own — that is the most important; second, the composer must have in his background some sense of musical culture and, if possible, a basis in folk or popular art; and third, a superstructure of organized musical activities must exist — that is, to some extent, at least — at the service of the native composer.

In both North and South America it was only natural that from the beginning the musical pattern followed lines which are normal for lands that are colonized by Europeans. In both Americas there was first the wilderness and the struggle merely to keep alive. Our Latin American cousins were more fortunate than we in their musical beginnings. Some of the Catholic missionaries from Spain were cultivated musicians intent upon teaching the rudiments of music to their charges. Pedro de Gante, a Franciscan padre, is credited with having started the first music school in the New World around 1524. He taught the natives to sing hymns and to write musical notation. The Puritan Fathers, on the other hand, were reported as downright unfriendly to the musical muse, although this harsh judgment has been somewhat tempered in recent years.

79

Nevertheless, it is safe to assume that apart from the singing of psalms there exist few if any signs that music as an art was encouraged.

It was during the later years of the colonial period of both North and South America that the first native, primitive composers raised their voices. These were mostly men who wrote their music in their spare time, as an avocation rather than as a profession. They, in turn, were soon aided by the initial influx of a certain number of professional musicians from abroad. In our own country many of these immigrants came at first from England. As Otto Kinkeldey has pointed out, in those days practically all our music came by way of England: Handel, Haydn, Mozart were known to the United States because they were known in England. A later wave came to our shores from Central Europe, especially Germany; and as a result our musical thinking was dominated for a great many years by Teutonic ideals. In Latin America the immigrant musician came principally from the Iberian Peninsula, as might be expected, while a later wave brought a large number of musical recruits from Italy.

Is there anything imaginative about the music composed in the Americas during the eighteenth and nineteenth centuries? So far as we can tell from the preserved records, very little. A few hardy primitives from the Revolutionary War period, like William Billings, have survived. Billings was a tanner by trade who ended up as a composer of hymn tunes and short patriotic pieces that only recently have been rediscovered and republished. They break harmonic rules occasionally and are sometimes a bit stiff in their contrapuntal joints, but despite that they have a rough honesty about them that keeps them alive for present-day listeners. Mention ought to be made of two other composers of the middle nineteenth century: Louis Moreau Gottschalk of New Orleans and Carlos Gomes of Rio de Janeiro. Both of them achieved fame abroad. Gottschalk led the life of a traveling piano virtuoso in the Lisztian manner. His importance historically comes from the fact that he is the earliest composer we know of who based his compositions on what are loosely called Latin American rhythms. It is only the exceptional piece of Gottschalk's that is of original quality; others are too obviously designed to dazzle the paying public. Nevertheless, he represents the first North American composer who made us aware of the rich source material to be derived from music of Hispanic origins. Carlos Gomes was a very successful opera composer, whose best works were performed at La Scala in Milan. His libretti were based on native Brazilian subject matter, but the musical style in which they were treated was indistinguishable from the Italian models on which they were based. Gomes was, however, the first of his kind and remains to this day a national hero in his own country.

We have our own national hero in Stephen Foster. He was a song writer rather than a composer, but he had a naturalness and sweetness of sentiment that transformed his melodies into the equivalent of folk song. His simplicity and sincerity are not easily imitated, but it is that same simplicity and naturalness that has inspired certain types of our own music in the twentieth century. Billings and Foster have no exact counterparts in the music of the southern hemisphere. The closest parallel will be found in the work of two Latin Americans who were active toward the end of the last century — Julián Aguirre in Argentina and Ignacio Cervantes in Cuba. They both composed a type of sensitive, almost Chopinesque, piano piece with a Creole flavor, that was to be followed by so many others in the same manner in Latin America. Aguirre and Cervantes give us the little piece in its pristine state, with a kind of disingenuous charm, before it was cheapened by the sentimentalities of numerous lesser composers.

If, as you see, the pickings are slim in the field of composed music of serious pretensions during the eighteenth and nineteenth centuries, there is a compensatory richness of invention when we turn to the popular forms of music making. It is not surprising that this should be so. Popular music crystallizes long in advance of composed concert music. After all, it reflects an unpremeditated and spontaneous welling up of musical emotion that requires no training and no musical superstructure. The human voice, with perhaps a drum or a simple folk instrument as accompaniment, is all that is needed to express a wide gamut of feelings. Folk music in the Western Hemisphere awaits some master investigator who can survey what is an immense terrain, and sort out and collate similarities and differences in such a way as to illuminate this whole field for us. I myself am far from being expert in this area, but I do retain vivid impressions of an unbelievably rich and comparatively little known territory of folk expression in Latin America.

I should like, parenthetically, to mention briefly a few examples that come to mind. The Cuban *guajira* is one of these. It is a form of country music of the Cuban farmer. Over the strumming of a few simple guitar chords the singer tells a tale in a singular style of melodious recitative that is drenched in individuality. It seems to me it could be listened to for hours on end. The same holds true for the deeply nostalgic music of the Peruvian Indian, played on ancient flutes, sometimes in pairs and with a curious heterophony — of an indescribable sadness. The exhilarating rhythm of the *bambuco* as it is danced in Colombia epitomizes the many popular dance patterns that alternate six-eight and three-quarter metrics with delightful effect. And I cannot mention dancing without remembering the incredible *frevo* as I saw it "performed" in the streets of Pernambuco. Musically the *frevo* demonstrates what occurs when the naïve musical mind seizes upon a well-known form — in this case the ordinary street march — and transforms it into a completely Afro-Brazilian manifestation. A similar transformation is worked upon the figurations of a Czerny piano exercise when a Cuban composer of popular music writes a *danzon*. Here pseudo elegance is the keynote — an "elegance" of high life in the Havana of 1905. As a final example I must mention the urban tango as one hears it in Argentina, played in a hard-as-nails manner by several accordions and a few assorted strings. This instrumental combination produces a sonority of knife-edge sharpness, so that even the would-be sentimental sections are played without a glimmer of sentimentality.

These different forms of folk and popular music briefly listed here must stand for many others. Diverting and interesting as they are, however, they are not what my musician friend was referring to when he inquired after signs of imaginativeness in the music of the Western world. Confining ourselves to serious music, there seems to me no doubt that if we are to lay claim to thinking inventively in the music of the Americas our principal stake must be a rhythmic one.

For some years now rhythm has been thought to be a special province of the music of both Americas. Roy Harris pointed this out a long time ago when he wrote: "Our rhythmic sense is less symmetrical than the European rhythmic sense. European musicians are trained to think of rhythm in its largest common denominator, while we are born with a feeling for its smallest units . . . We do not employ unconventional rhythms as a sophistical gesture; we cannot avoid them . . ." Let us see if it is possible to make more precise these remarks of Harris' — whether it is possible to track down the source and nature of these so-called American rhythms.

Most commentators are agreed that the source of our rhythmic habits of mind are partly African and partly Spanish. Since the Iberian peninsula was itself a melting pot of many races, with a strong admixture of Arab culture from Africa, the Iberian and African influences are most certainly interrelated. In certain countries the aboriginal Indians have contributed something through their own traditional rhythmic patterns, although this remains rather conjectural. As time goes on, it becomes more and more difficult to disengage the African from the Iberian influence. We speak of Afro-Cuban, Afro-Brazilian, Afro-American rhythms in an attempt to circumvent this difficulty. Since Spain and Portugal have, by

83

themselves, produced nothing like the rhythmic developments of the Western countries, it is only natural to conclude that we owe the vitality and interest of our rhythms in large measure to the Negro in his new environment. It is impossible to imagine what American music would have been like if the slave trade had never been instituted in North and South America. The slave ships brought a precious cargo of wonderfully gifted musicians, with an instinctive feeling for the most complex rhythmic pulsations. The strength of that musical impulse is attested to by the fact that it is just as alive today in the back streets of Rio de Janeiro or Havana or New Orleans as it was two hundred years ago. Recent recordings of musical rites among certain African tribes of today make perfectly apparent the direct musical line that connects the Náñigos of today's Cuba or Brazil with their forefathers of the African forest.

What is the nature of this gift? First, a conception of rhythm not as mental exercise but as something basic to the body's rhythmic impulse. This basic impulse is exteriorized with an insistence that knows no measure, ranging from a self-hypnotic monotony to a riotous frenzy of subconsciously controlled poundings. Second, an unparalleled ingenuity in the spinning out of unequal metrical units in the unadorned rhythmic line. And lastly, and most significant, a polyrhythmic structure arrived at through the combining of strongly independent blocks of sound. No European music I ever heard has even approached the rhythmic intensities obtained by five different drummers, each separately hammering out his own pattern of sound, so that they enmesh one with another to produce a most complex metrical design. Oriental musics contain subtle cross-rhythms of polyrhythmic implication, but we of the Americas learned our rhythmic lessons largely from the Negro. Put thus baldly it may be said, with some justice perhaps, that I am oversimplifying. But even if I overstate the case the fact remains that the rhythmic life in the scores of Roy Harris, William Schuman, Marc Blitzstein, and a host

84

of other representative American composers is indubitably linked to Negroid sources of rhythm.

A very different idea of the polymetric organization of pulsations is familiar in European music. How could it be otherwise? Any music which is contrapuntally conceived is likely to have melodic lines that imply different rhythms, and these would naturally be heard simultaneously. But the point here is one of emphasis and degree. Few musicians would argue that the classical composers wrote music that was polyrhythmically arranged, in the sense in which I am using the term here. Mozart and Brahms were far from being constrained by the bar line, as is made clear by certain remarkable sections of rhythmic ingenuity in their scores, and yet their normal procedure with rhythm implies a regularity and evenness of metrical design that we think of as typical of Western music.

Other examples of Western music, especially in choral literature, demonstrate an unconventional rhythmic organization. But for the purpose I have in mind it will suffice to confine ourselves to two kinds of music, before the twentieth century, which appear to me to be exceptional in this respect, that is, in their concentration on polyrhythmic texture: the recently deciphered scores of French and Italian composers at the end of the thirteen hundreds; and the English madrigals of Shakespeare's day. Exceptional as these are, I hope to show that American rhythms are premised upon a quite different type of polymetrics — a conception that is nowhere else duplicated.

The composers of the late fourteenth century — some of whose music has recently been made available through a publication of the Mediaeval Academy of America — exhibit in their ballades and virelais a most astonishing intricacy of rhythmic play. The editor of the volume in question, Willi Apel, suggests that these rhythms may not have been entirely "felt" by their composers, but were perhaps the result of "notational speculation." It is quite possible that their system of notation provided these composers with a new toy by means of which they were enabled to experiment with all manner of unprecedented rhythmic combinations. But even as mere paper rhythms — and it is certainly doubtful whether they are only that — they hold great fascination for the present-day musician.

The rhythmic complexities of the Elizabethan madrigalists, on the other hand, were firmly grounded in English speech rhythms. By retaining these independently in each vocal part a delightful freedom of cross-rhythmic irregularities resulted. And since English is a strongly accented language — with qualitative rather than quantitative values — a rich and supple variety of rhythm was obtained that no other European school of that time could match. Curiously enough, it is only in the twentieth century that the rhythmic skill of the Elizabethans has come to be understood and appreciated. Formerly the very freedom of their metrical designs was thought to be a fault rather than a virtue. Wilfrid Mellers sums this up when he writes: ". . . the sixteenth century, which nineteenth century commentators considered rhythmically 'vague,' actually developed rhythm to the highest point it has reached in European history." And he adds: "Perhaps it is no accident that in England this supreme development of musical rhythm coincides with the development of mature Shakespearean blank verse, which achieves its effect from a delicate tension between speech rhythm and metrical accent."

It is important to point out that the polyrhythmic structures of the Elizabethan composers are different in kind from those that typify American music. They were concerned with the creation of a supple and fluid pulse in which no single strong beat dominated the over-all rhythmic flow. Our polyrhythms are more characteristically the deliberate setting, one against the other, of a steady pulse with a free pulse. Its most familiar manifestation is in the small jazz band combination, where the so-called rhythm section provides the ground metrics around which the melody instruments can freely invent rhythms of their own. Added to this influence from popular sources was the general concentration on rhythmic intensities for which our century is notable. The interest in national musics of different kinds — Russian, Hungarian, Scandinavian — with their unconventional rhythms acted as further stimulus in the breaking down of the tyranny of the bar line. Rhythmic factors became one of the preponderant concerns of serious music in most European countries.

In the Americas, however, the typical feature of our own rhythms was this juxtaposition of steadiness, either implied or actually heard, as against freedom of rhythmic invention. Take, for example, the stylistic device of "swinging" a tune. This simply means that over a steady ground rhythm the singer or instrumentalists toy with the beat, never being exactly *on* it, but either anticipating it or lagging behind it in gradations of metrical units so subtle that our notational system has no way of indicating it. Of course you cannot stay off the beat unless you know where that beat is. Here again freedom is interesting only in relation to regularity. On the other hand, when our better jazz bands wish to be rhythmically exact they come down on the beat with a trip-hammer precision that puts our symphonic musicians to shame. Thus an *ambiance* of playing fast and loose with the rhythm is encouraged which has tended to separate more and more the American and European conception of musical pulse.

The European is taught to think of rhythm as applying always to a phrase of music — as the articulation of that phrase. We, on the contrary, are not averse to thinking of rhythm as disembodied, so to speak, as if it were a frame to which certain tones might be added as an afterthought. This is, of course, not meant to be taken as literally true, but merely indicates a tendency on our part to think of rhythms as separately pulsating quarter or eighth or sixteenth notes — what Roy Harris means when he says we feel at ease with rhythm's "smallest units." Small units, when combined, are likely to add up to musically unconventional totals of five, seven, or

87

eleven by contrast with the more familiar combinations of two plus two, or of three plus three. Our European colleagues may protest and claim: "But we too write our music nowadays with the freedom of unequal divisions of the bar lines." Of course they do; but nonetheless it is only necessary to hear a well-trained European musician performing American rhythms to perceive the difference in rhythmic conceptions.

Winthrop Sargeant was making a similar point in terms of the jazz player when he wrote: "The jazz musician has a remarkable sense of subdivided and subordinate accents in what he is playing, even though it be the slowest sort of jazz. This awareness of minute component metrical units shows itself in all sorts of syncopative subtleties that are quite foreign to European music. It is, I think," he adds, "the lack of this awareness in most European 'classical' musicians that explains their well-known inability to play jazz in a convincing manner."

The special concern with rhythm that is characteristic of American music has had, as an offshoot, a rather more than usual interest in percussive sounds, as such. Orchestras, as constituted in the nineteenth century had only a comparatively few elementary noise-making instruments to draw upon. In recent times the native musics of Cuba, Brazil, and Mexico have greatly enriched our percussive gamut through the addition of an entire battery of noise-making instruments peculiar to those countries. Some of these are slowly finding their way into our more conventional musical organizations. New and distinctive sounds and noises have been added to what was formerly the most neglected department in the symphony orchestra. A departure from routine thinking occurred when contemporary composers began to write for groups of percussion instruments alone. Edgar Varèse was a pioneer in that field in the twenties and his example encouraged other composers to experiment along similar lines. I suppose we may consider Béla Bartók's Sonata for two pianos and two percussion players and Stravinsky's orchestration of his choral ballet *Les Noces* for four pianos and thirteen percussion players as further proof that an interest in unusual sonorities is typical of our times. But it is the musicians of North and Latin America who come by this interest most naturally, and from whom we may expect a continuing inventiveness and curiosity as to the percussive sound. Villa-Lobos once aroused my envy by showing me his personal collection of native Brazilian percussion instruments. After a visit like that, one asks oneself: how did we ever manage to get along for so long a time with the bare boom of the bass drum and the obvious crash of the cymbals?

Before leaving the subject of rhythm-inspired music something should be said of a specialty of the jazz musician that has been greatly admired, particularly by the European enthusiast. I refer, of course, to the improvisatory powers of the popular performer. If one looks up the word "improvisation" in the music dictionaries, reference will be made to the ability of composers, at certain periods of musical history, to improvise entire compositions in contrapuntal style. The art of improvising an accompaniment from a figured bass line was an ordinary accomplishment for the well-trained keyboard instrumentalist during the baroque period. But the idea of *group* improvisation was reserved for the jazz age. What gives it more than passing interest is the phonograph, for it is the phonograph that makes it possible to preserve and thereby savor the fine flavor of what is necessarily a lucky chance result. It is especially this phase of our popular music that has caused the French *aficionado* to become lyrical about *le jazz hot*.

When you improvise it is axiomatic that you take risks and can't foretell results. When five or six musicians improvise simultaneously the result is even more fortuitous. That is its charm. The improvising performer is the very antithesis of that tendency in contemporary composition that demands absolute exactitude in the execution of the printed page. Perhaps Mr. Stravinsky and those who support his view of rigorous control for the performer have been trying to sit

89

on the lid too hard. Perhaps the performer should be given more elbow room and a greater freedom of improvisatory choice. A young composer recently conceived the novel idea of writing a "composition" on graph paper which indicated where a chord was to be placed in space and when in time, but left to the performer freedom to choose whatever chords happened to strike his fancy at the moment of execution. Most jazz improvisers are not entirely free either, partly because of the conventionality of jazz harmonic formulas, and partly because of over-used melodic formulas. Recent examples of group improvisations by Lennie Tristano and some few other jazz men are remarkable precisely because they avoid both these pitfalls. When American musicians improvise thus freely, and we are able to rehear their work through recordings, the European musician is the first to agree that something has been developed here that has no duplication abroad.

If Negro and Iberian source materials have exerted a strong hold on the imagination of musicians in the Americas, the influence of the musical culture of the aboriginal Indians seems to have been slight. Tragically little has survived from the music of pre-Columbian civilizations, and what there is comes to us in the form of a few instruments, and the scales that may be deduced from some of them. The Indians of today, when they sing and dance, produce a music that is difficult to authenticate. How much of what they do is the result of oral tradition and how much acquired from the circumstances of their post-Conquest environment is difficult to say. Their influence on serious music has been strongest in those countries where Indian culture was most highly developed and has been best preserved, such as Mexico and Peru. In our own country, where the Indian had not reached the cultural level of the Incas or Aztecs, only a few composers were hopeful of finding stimulus in the thematic materials available to them. Despite the efforts of Arthur Farwell and his group of composer friends, and despite the *Indian Suite* of Edward MacDowell, nothing really fructifying resulted. It is understandable that the first Americans would have a sentimental attraction for our composers, especially at a time when the American composer himself was searching for some indigenous musical expression. But our composers were obviously incapable of identifying themselves sufficiently with such primitive source materials as to make these convincing when heard out of context.

The contemporary Chilean composer, Carlos Isamitt, was more successful in a somewhat analogous situation. The Araucanian Indians of southern Chile are not a highly developed people like the Incas of Peru, and yet Isamitt, by living among them and immersing himself in their culture, was able to draw something of their independent spirit into his own symphonic settings of their songs and dances.

But the principal imprint of the Indian personality — its deepest reflection in the music of our hemisphere — is to be found in the present-day school of Mexican composers, and especially in the work of Carlos Chavez and Silvestre Revueltas. With them it is not so much a question of themes as it is of character. Even without previous knowledge of the Amerindian man, his essential nature may be inferred from their scores. The music of Chavez is strong and deliberate, at times almost fatalistic in tone; it bespeaks the sober and stolid and lithic Amerindian. It is music of persistence — relentless and uncompromising; there is nothing of the humble Mexican peon here. It is music that knows its own mind — stark and clear and, if one may say so, earthy in an abstract way. There are no frills, nothing extraneous; it is like the bare wall of an adobe hut, which can be so expressive by virtue of its inexpressivity. Chavez' music is, above all, profoundly non-European. To me it possesses an Indian quality that is at the same time curiously contemporary in spirit. Sometimes it strikes me as the most truly contemporary music I know, not in the superficial sense, but in the sense that it comes closest to expressing the fundamental reality of modern man after he has been stripped of the accumulations of centuries of aesthetic experiences.

It is illuminating to contrast the work of Chavez with that of his countryman, the late Silvestre Revueltas, whose vibrant, tangy scores sing of a more colorful, perhaps a more mestizo side of the Mexican character. Revueltas was a man of the people, with a wonderfully keen ear for the sounds of the people's music. He wrote no large symphonies or sonatas, but many short orchestral sketches with fanciful names such as *Ventanas, Esquinas, Janitzio* (*Windows, Corners, Janitzio*) — the last named after the little island in Lake Pátzcuaro. His list of compositions would be longer than it is, were it not for the fact that he died when he was forty years old, in 1940. But the pieces that he left us are crowded with an abundance and vitality — a Mexican abundance and vitality — that make them a pleasure to hear.

In seeking for qualities of the specifically Western imagination it seems to me that there are two composers of South and North America who share many traits in common, and especially a certain richness and floridity of invention that has no exact counterpart in Europe. I am thinking of the Brazilian, Heitor Villa-Lobos, and of the American from Connecticut, Charles Ives.

Leaving aside questions of relative value, it seems to me one would have to turn to Herman Melville's biblical prose or the oceanic verse of Walt Whitman to find an analogous largess. Is it illusory to connect this munificence of imagination in both composers with the scope and freedom of a new world? They share also the main drawback of an overabundant imagination: the inability to translate the many images that crowd their minds into scores of a single and unified vision. In the case of Villa-Lobos there is strong temptation to identify his crowded imagination with the luxuriance of a jungle landscape; the very sound of the music suggests it. In Ives we sense the strain of reaching for the transcendental and the universal that was native to his part of America.

Do both Ives and Villa-Lobos suffer from an inflated style? Alexis de Tocqueville, who visited our shores in the eighteen thirties, reported that the "inflated style" was typical for American orators and writers. There must be something about big countries — Brazil, in case you've forgotten, is larger than territorial United States — something that encourages creative artists to expand themselves beyond all normal limits. The lack of restraint made customary by tradition plays a role here. And when that lack of restraint is combined with a copious and fertile imagination they together seem to engender a concomitant lack of self-criticism. Is it at all possible to be carefully selective if one possesses no traditional standard of reference? It would hardly seem so. The power in both men comes through in spite of their inability, at times, to exercise critical self-judgment. It is a power of originality of a curiously indigenous kind that makes their music appear to be so profoundly of this hemisphere.

There exist several parallelisms between the work of Ives and of Villa-Lobos. At one point in their careers they both used impressionistic methods to suggest realistic scenes of local life. With this there was the tendency to give their pieces homespun titles: Ives's symphonic picture of the *Housatonic at Stockbridge* is matched by Villa-Lobos' *Little Train of Caipira*. Both men have a love for trying to make the "specific richly symbolic of the universal." They both were technically adventurous, experimenting with polytonal and polyrhythmic effects long before they had had contact with European examples of these new resources. (Ives was especially remarkable in this respect.) And they both retain central positions in the history of their country's music because of their willingness to ignore academic European models which for so long had satisfied other composers in their respective lands. And yet, in spite of these many similarities, it is characteristic that their music is utterly personal and distinct, one from the other.

In strong contrast to the floridity and occasional grandiloquence of Ives and Villa-Lobos, but no less representative of another and different aspect of America, is the music of Virgil Thomson and Douglas Moore. There is nothing in serious European music that is quite like it — nothing so downright plain and bare as their commerce with simple tunes and square rhythms and Sunday-school harmonies. Evocative of the homely virtues of rural America, their work may be said to constitute a "midwestern style" in American music. Attracted by the unadorned charm of a revivalist hymn, or a sentimental ditty, or a country dance, they give us the musical counterpart of a regionalism that is familiar in our literature and painting but is seldom found in our symphonies and concertos. Both these men, needless to say, are sophisticated musicians, so that their frank acceptance of so limited a musical vocabulary is a gesture of faith in their own heritage. Both have best exploited this type of midwestern pseudo primitivism in their operas and film scores. Thomson especially, with the aid of Gertrude Stein's texts in *Four Saints in Three Acts* and *The Mother of Us All,* has succeeded in giving a highly original twist to the disarming simplicities of his musical materials. Here, in a new guise, it should be recalled, is an idea of earlier American composers like Gilbert and Farwell, who believed that only by emphasizing our own crude musical realities, and resisting the blandishments of the highly developed musical cultures of other peoples, would we ever find our own indigenous musical speech.

I realize that there are undoubtedly among my readers those who disapprove heartily of this searching for "Americanisms" in the works of our contemporaries. Roger Sessions, Walter Piston, and Samuel Barber are composers whose works are not strikingly "American" in the special sense of this chapter, and yet a full summary of the American imagination at work in music — such as this

94

discussion does not pretend to be — would naturally stress the import of their work. There is a universalist ideal, exemplified by their symphonies and chamber music, that belittles the nationalistic note and stresses "predominately musical values." I myself lose patience with the European music lover who wants our music to be all new, brand-new, absolutely different. They forget that we are, as Waldo Frank once put it, the "grave of Europe," by which I suppose he meant to suggest that we have inherited everything they are and know; and we shall have to absorb it and make it completely our own before we can hope for the unadulterated American creation. Nevertheless, there is a deep psychological need to look for present signs of that creation. I know this to be true from my own reactions to the music of other nations, especially nations whose music is still unformed, for we inevitably look for the note that makes it characteristically itself. This attitude may be narrow and wrong, but it is an unpremeditated reaction which rightfully should be balanced by the realization that not all the composers of any country are to be limited to an obviously indigenous expression.

In a lecture delivered sometime before 1907, the American composer Edward MacDowell said: "What we must arrive at is the youthful optimistic vitality and the undaunted tenacity of spirit that characterizes the American man. That is what I hope to see echoed in American music." I think MacDowell's hope has been fulfilled — partly, at least — for if there is a school of American composers, optimism is certainly its keynote. But the times have caught up with us, and already mere optimism seems insufficient. If it is not to be mere boyish exuberance it must be tempered, as it is in the work of our best composers, by a reflection of the American man, not as MacDowell knew him at the turn of the century, but as he appears to us with all his complex world about him. Imagination will be needed to echo that man in music.

CHAPTER SIX

The Composer
in Industrial America

IS IT SHEER CHANCE, I sometimes wonder, that no one has ever published an adequate critical summary of the whole field of American serious composition? There are, of course, several compendiums containing mostly biographical data and lists of works, but no one has yet attempted to summarize what our composers have accomplished, nor to say what it feels like to be a composer in industrial America. What sort of creative life the composer leads, what his relation to the community is or should be — these and many other interesting facets of the composer's life have hardly been explored.

My colleague, the American composer Elliott Carter, once said to me that in his opinion only an imaginative mind could possibly conceive itself a composer of serious music in an industrial community like the United States. Actually it seems to me that we Americans who compose alternate between states of mind that make composition appear to be the most natural and ordinary pursuit and other moods when it seems completely extraneous to the primary interests of our industrial environment. By temperament I lean to the side that considers composing in our community as a natural force — something to be taken for granted — rather than the freakish occupation of a very small minority of our citizens.

And yet, judging the situation dispassionately, I can see that we ought not to take it for granted. We must examine the place of the artist and composer in our kind of society, partly to take account of its effect on the artist and also as a commentary on our society itself. The fact is that an industrial society must prove itself capable of producing creative artists of stature, for its inability to do so would be a serious indictment of the fundamental tenets of that society.

From the moment that one doesn't take composing for granted in our country, a dozen questions come to mind. What *is* the composer's life in America? Does it differ so very much from that of the European or even the Latin American composer of today? Or from the life of United States composers in other periods? Are our objectives and purposes the same as they always have been? These questions and many related ones are continually being written about by the literary critic, but they are infrequently dealt with in the musical world. I can best consider them by relating them to my own experience as a creative artist in America. Generalizing from that experience it may be possible to arrive at certain conclusions. This engenders an autobiographical mood, but it is impossible to avoid it if I am to use myself as guinea pig.

My own experience I think of as typical because I grew up in an urban community (in my case, New York City) and lived in an environment that had little or no connection with serious music. My discovery of music was rather like coming upon an unsuspected city — like discovering Paris or Rome if you had never before heard of their existence. The excitement of discovery was enhanced because I came upon only a few streets at a time, but before long I began to suspect the full extent of this city. The instinctual drive toward the world of sound must have been very strong in my case, since it triumphed over a commercially minded environment that, so far as I could tell, had never given a thought to art or to art expression as a way of life.

Scenes come back to me from my early high school years. I see myself digging out scores from the dusty upstairs shelves of the old Brooklyn Public Library on Montague Street; here were riches of which my immediate neighbors were completely unaware. Those were the impressionable years of exploration. I recall nights at home alone singing to myself the songs of Hugo Wolf — living on a plane which had no parallel in the rest of my daily life. Or explaining to a school friend, after hearing one of my first orchestral concerts in the Brooklyn Academy of Music, in the days before radio and recorded symphonies, what a large orchestra sounded like. I've forgotten my exact description except for the punch line: "And then, and then," I said, after outlining how the instrumental forces were gradually marshaled little by little, "and then — the whole ORchestra came in." This was musical glory manifesting itself. Most of all I remember the first time I openly admitted to another human being that I intended to become a composer of music. To set oneself up as a rival of the masters: what a daring and unheard-of project for a Brooklyn youth! It was summer time and I was fifteen years old — and the friend who heard this startling confession might have laughed at me. Fortunately, he didn't.

The curious thing, in retrospect, is the extent to which I was undisturbed by the ordinariness of the workaday world about me. It didn't occur to me to revolt against its crassness, for in the last analysis it was the only world I knew, and I simply accepted it for what it was. Music for me was not a refuge or a consolation; it merely gave meaning to my own existence, where the world outside had little or none. I couldn't help feeling a little sorry for those to whom music and art in general meant nothing, but that was their own concern. As for myself, I could not imagine my own life without it.

It seems to me now, some thirty-five years later, that music and the life about me did not touch. Music was like the inside of a great building that shut out the street noises. They were the noises natural to a street; but it was good to have the quiet of the great building available, not as a haven or a hiding place, but as a different and more meaningful place.

Here at the start, I imagine, is a first difference from the European musician, whose contacts with serious music, even when delayed, must seem entirely natural, since "classical music" is German, English, French, Italian, and so forth — has roots, in other words, in the young composer's own background. In my America, "classical" music was a foreign importation. But the foreignness of serious music did not trouble me at all in those days: my early preoccupations were with technique and expressivity. I found that I derived profound satisfaction from exteriorizing inner feelings — at times, surprisingly concrete ones — and giving them shape. The scale on which I worked at first was small — two or three page piano pieces or songs — but the intensity of feeling was real. It must have been the reality of this inner intensity I speak of which produced the conviction that I was capable of some day writing a longer, and perhaps, significant work. There is no other way of explaining a young artist's self-assurance. It is not founded on faith alone (and of course there can be no certainty about it), but some real kernel there must be, from which the later work will grow.

My years in Europe from the age of twenty to twenty-three made me acutely conscious of the origins of the music I loved. Most of the time I spent in France, where the characteristics of French culture are evident at every turn. The relation of French music to the life around me became increasingly manifest. Gradually, the idea that my personal expression in music ought somehow to be related to my own back-home environment took hold of me. The conviction grew inside me that the two things that seemed always to have been so separate in America — music and the life about me — must be made to touch. This desire to make the music I wanted to write come out of the life I had lived in America became a preoccupation of mine in the twenties. It was not so very different from the experience of other young American artists, in other fields, who had gone abroad to study in that period; in greater or lesser degree, all of us discovered America in Europe.

In music our problem was a special one: it really began when we started to search for what Van Wyck Brooks calls a usable past. In those days the example of our American elders in music was not readily at hand. Their music was not often played except perhaps locally. Their scores were seldom published, and even when published, were expensive and not easily available to the inquiring student. We knew, of course, that they too had been to Europe as students, absorbing musical culture, principally in Teutonic centers of learning. Like us, they came home full of admiration for the treasures of European musical art, with the self-appointed mission of expounding these glories to their countrymen.

But when I think of these older men, and especially of the most important among them — John Knowles Paine, George Chadwick, Arthur Foote, Horatio Parker — who made up the Boston school of composers at the turn of the century, I am aware of a fundamental difference between their attitude and our own. Their attitude was founded upon an admiration for the European art work and an identification with it that made the seeking out of any other art formula a kind of sacrilege. The challenge of the Continental art work was not: can we do better or can we also do something truly our own, but merely, can we do as well. But of course one never does "as well." Meeting Brahms or Wagner on his own terms one is certain to come off second best. They loved the masterworks of Europe's mature culture not like creative personalities but like the schoolmasters that many of them became. They accepted an artistic authority that came from abroad, and seemed intent on conforming to that authority.

I do not mean to underestimate what they accomplished for the beginnings of serious American musical composition. Quite the contrary. Within the framework of the German musical tradition

in which most of them had been trained, they composed industri-
ously, they set up professional standards of workmanship, and encouraged a seriousness of purpose in their students that long out-
lasted their own activities. But judged purely on their merits as
composers, estimable though their symphonies and operas and
chamber works are, they were essentially practitioners in the conventional idiom of their own day, and therefore had little to offer
us of a younger generation. No doubt it is trite to say so, but it is
none the less true, I think, that a genteel aura hangs about them.
There were no Dostoyevskys, no Rimbauds among them; no one
expired in the gutter like Edgar Allan Poe. It may not be gracious
to say so, but I fear that the New England group of composers of
that time were in all their instincts overgentlemanly, too well-man-
nered, and their culture reflected a certain museumlike propriety
and bourgeois solidity.

In some strange way Edward MacDowell, a contemporary of
theirs, managed to escape some of the pitfalls of the New Englanders. Perhaps the fact that he had been trained from an early
age in the shadow of the *Conservatoire* at Paris and had spent many
subsequent years abroad gave him a familiarity in the presence of
Europe's great works that the others never acquired. This is pure
surmise on my part; but it is fairly obvious that, speaking generally, his music shows more independence of spirit, and certainly
more personality than was true of his colleagues around 1900. It
was the music of MacDowell, among Americans, that we knew
best, even in 1925. I cannot honestly say that we dealt kindly with
his work at that period; his central position as "foremost composer
of his generation" made him especially apt as a target for our impatience with the weaknesses and orthodoxies of an older generation. Nowadays, although his music is played less often than it
once was, one can appreciate more justly what MacDowell had: a
sensitive and individual poetic gift, and a special turn of harmony
of his own. He is most successful when he is least pretentious. It

seems likely that for a long time MacDowell's name will be secure in the annals of American music, even though his direct influence as a composer can hardly be found in present-day American music.

The search for a usable past, for musical ancestors, led us to examine most closely, as was natural, the music of the men who immediately preceded our own time — the generation that was active after the death of MacDowell in 1908. It was not until about that period that some of our composers were able to shake off the all-pervasive German influence in American music. With Debussy and Ravel, France had reappeared as a world figure on the international musical scene, and French impressionism became the new influence. Composers like Charles Martin Loeffler and Charles T. Griffes were the radicals of their day. But we see now that if the earlier Boston composers were prone to take refuge in the sure values of the academic world, these newer men were in danger of escaping to a kind of artistic ivory tower. As composers, they seemed quite content to avoid contact with the world they lived in. Unlike the poetry of Sandburg or the novels of Dreiser or Frank Norris, so conscious of the crude realities of industrial America, you will find no picture of the times in the music of Loeffler or Griffes. The danger was that their music would become a mere adjunct to the grim realities of everyday life, a mere exercise in polite living. They loved the picturesque, the poetic, the exotic — medievalisms, Hinduisms, Gregorian chants, *chinoiseries*. Even their early critics stressed the "decadent" note in their music.

Despite this *fin-de-siècle* tendency, Charles Griffes is a name that deserves to be remembered. He represents a new type of composer as contrasted with the men of Boston. Griffes was just an ordinary small-town boy from Elmira, New York. He never knew the important musical people of his time and he never managed to get a better job than that of music teacher in a private school for boys, outside Tarrytown, New York. And yet there are pages in his music where we recognize the presence of the truly inspired moment. His was the work of a sentient human being, forward-looking, for its period, with a definite relationship to the impressionists and to Scriabin. No one can say how far Griffes might have developed if his career had not been cut short by death in his thirty-sixth year, in 1920. What he gave those of us who came after him was a sense of the adventurous in composition, of being thoroughly alive to the newest trends in world music and to the stimulus that might be derived from such contact.

Looking backward for first signs of the native composer with an interest in the American scene one comes upon the sympathetic figure of Henry F. Gilbert. His special concern was the use of Negro material as a basis for serious composition. This idea had been given great impetus by the arrival in America in 1892 of the Bohemian composer, Antonin Dvořák. His writing of the New World Symphony *in* the new world, using melodic material strongly suggestive of Negro spirituals, awakened a desire on the part of several of the younger Americans of that era to write music of local color, characteristic of one part, at least, of the American scene. Henry Gilbert was a Boston musician, but he had little in common with his fellow New Englanders, for it was his firm conviction that it was better to write a music in one's own way, no matter how modest and restricted its style might be, than to compose large works after a foreign model. Gilbert thought he had solved the problem of an indigenous expression by quoting Negro or Creole themes in his overtures and ballets. What he did was suggestive on a primitive and pioneering level, but the fact is that he lacked the technique and musicianship for expressing his ideals in a significant way.

What, after all, does it mean to make use of a hymn tune or a cowboy tune in a serious musical composition? There is nothing inherently pure in a melody of folk source that cannot be effectively spoiled by a poor setting. The use of such materials ought never to be a mechanical process. They can be successfully handled only by a composer who is able to identify himself with, and reëxpress in his own terms, the underlying emotional connotation of the material. A hymn tune represents a certain order of feeling: simplicity, plainness, sincerity, directness. It is the reflection of those qualities in a stylistically appropriate setting, imaginative and unconventional and not mere quotation, that gives the use of folk tunes reality and importance. In the same way, to transcribe the cowboy tune so that its essential quality is preserved is a task for the imaginative composer with a professional grasp of the problem.

In any event, we in the twenties were little influenced by the efforts of Henry Gilbert, for the truth is that we were after bigger game. Our concern was not with the quotable hymn or spiritual: we wanted to find a music that would speak of universal things in a vernacular of American speech rhythms. We wanted to write music on a level that left popular music far behind — music with a largeness of utterance wholly representative of the country that Whitman had envisaged.

Through a curious quirk of musical history the man who was writing such a music — a music that came close to approximating our needs — was entirely unknown to us. I sometimes wonder whether the story of American music might have been different if Charles Ives and his work had been played at the time he was composing most of it — roughly the twenty years from 1900 to 1920. Perhaps not; perhaps he was too far in advance of his own generation. As it turned out, it was not until the thirties that he was discovered by the younger composers. As time goes on, Ives takes on a more and more legendary character, for his career as composer is surely unique not only in America but in musical history anywhere.

In the preceding chapter I mentioned the abundance of imagination in the music of Ives, its largeness of vision, its experimental side, and the composer's inability to be self-critical. Here I want to be more specific and stress not so much the mystical and transcendental side of his nature — the side that makes him most nearly akin to men like Thoreau and Emerson — but rather the element in his musical speech that accounts for his acceptance of the vernacular as an integral part of that speech. That acceptance, it seems to me, was a highly significant moment in our musical development.

Ives had an abiding interest in the American scene as lived in the region with which he was familiar. He grew up in Danbury, Connecticut, but completed his schooling at Yale University, where he graduated in 1898. Later he moved on to New York, where he spent many years as a successful man of business. Throughout his life one gets the impression that he was deeply immersed in his American roots. He was fascinated by typical features of New England small-town life: the village church choir, the Fourth of July celebration, the firemen's band, a barn dance, a village election, George Washington's Birthday. References to all these things and many similar ones can be found in his sonatas and symphonies. Ives treated this subject matter imaginatively rather than literally. Don't think for an instant that he was a mere provincial, with a happy knack for incorporating indigenous material into his many scores. No, Ives was an intellectual, and what is most impressive is not his evocation of a local landscape but the over-all range and comprehensiveness of his musical mind.

Nevertheless Ives had a major problem in attempting to achieve formal coherence in the midst of so varied a musical material. He did not by any means entirely succeed in this difficult assignment. At its worst his music is amorphous, disheveled, haphazard — like the music of a man who is incapable of organizing his many different thoughts. Simultaneity of impression was an idea that intrigued Ives all his life. As a boy he never got over the excitement of hearing three village bands play on different street corners at the same time. Ives tried a part solution for reproducing this simultaneity of effect which was subsequently dubbed "musical perspective"

105

by one music critic. He composed a work which is a good example of this device. It is called "Central Park in the Dark," dates from 1907, and, like many of Ives's work, is based on a poetic transcription of a realistic scene. The composer thought up a simple but ingenious method for picturing this scene, thereby enhancing what was in reality a purely musical intention. Behind a velvet curtain he placed a muted string orchestra to represent the sounds of the night, and before the curtain he placed a woodwind ensemble which made city noises. Together they evoke Central Park in the dark. The effect is almost that of musical cubism, since the music seems to exist independently on different planes. This so-called musical perspective makes use of musical realism in order to create an impressionistic effect.

The full stature of Ives as composer will not be known until we have an opportunity to judge his output as a whole. Up to now, only a part of his work has been deciphered and published. But whatever the total impression may turn out to be, his example in the twenties helped us not at all, for our knowledge of his work was sketchy — so little of it had been played.

Gradually, by the late twenties, our search for musical ancestors had been abandoned or forgotten, partly, I suppose, because we became convinced that there were none — that we had none. We were on our own, and something of the exhilaration that goes with being on one's own accompanied our every action. This self-reliant attitude was intensified by the open resistance to new music that was typical in the period after the First World War. Some of the opposition came from our elders — conservative composers who undoubtedly thought of us as noisy upstarts, carriers of dangerous ideas. The fun of the fight against the musical philistines, the sorties and strategies, the converts won, and the hot arguments with dull-witted critics partly explain the particular excitements of that period. Concerts of new music were a gamble: who could say whether Acario Catapos of Chile, or Josef Hauer of Vienna, or Kaikhosru

Sorabji of England was the coming man of the future? It was an adventuresome time — a time when fresh resources had come to music and were being tested by a host of new composers with energy and ebullient spirits.

Sometimes it seems to me that it was the composers who were the very last to take cognizance of a marked change that came over the musical scene after the stimulating decade of the twenties. The change was brought about, of course, by the introduction for the first time of the mass media of distribution in the field of music. First came the phonograph, then the radio, then the sound film, then the tape recorder, and now television. Composers were slow to realize that they were being faced with revolutionary changes: they were no longer merely writing their music within an industrial framework; industrialization itself had entered the framework of what had previously been our comparatively restricted musical life. One of the crucial questions of our times was injected: how are we to make contact with this enormously enlarged potential audience, without sacrificing in any way the highest musical standards?

Jacques Barzun recently called this question the problem of numbers. "A huge increase in the number of people, in the number of activities, and possibilities, of desires and satisfactions, is the great new fact." Composers are free to ignore this "great new fact" if they choose; no one is forcing them to take the large new public into account. But it would be foolish to side-step what is essentially a new situation in music: foolish because musical history teaches that when the audience changes, music changes. Our present condition is very analogous to that in the field of books. Readers are generally quick to distinguish between the book that is a best-seller by type and the book that is meant for the restricted audience of intellectuals. In between there is a considerable body of literature that appeals to the intelligent reader with broad interests. Isn't a similar situation likely to develop in music? Aren't you able even now to name a few best-seller compositions of recent vintage? Certainly the complex piece — the piece that is "born difficult" — is an entirely familiar musical manifestation. But it is the intelligent listener with broad interests who has tastes at the present time which are difficult to define. Composers may have to relinquish old thinking habits and become more consciously aware of the new audience for whom they are writing.

In the past, when I have proffered similar gratuitous advice on this subject, I have often been misinterpreted. Composers of abstruse music thought they were under attack, and claimed that complexities were natural to them — "born that way," a contention that I never meant to dispute. I was simply pointing out that certain modes of expression may not need the full gamut of post-tonal implications, and that certain expressive purposes can be appropriately carried out only by a simple texture in a basically tonal scheme. As I see it, music that is born complex is not inherently better or worse than music that is born simple.

Others took my meaning to be a justification for the watering down of their ideas for the purposes of making their works acceptable for mass consumption. Still others have used my own compositions to prove that I make a sharp distinction between those written in a "severe" and those in a "simple" style. The inference is sometimes drawn that I have consciously abandoned my earlier dissonant manner in order to popularize my style — and this notion is applauded enthusiastically; while those of a different persuasion are convinced that only my so-called "severe" style is really serious.

In my own mind there never was so sharp a dichotomy between the various works I have written. Different purposes produce different kinds of work, that is all. The new mechanization of music's media has emphasized functional requirements, very often in terms of a large audience. That need would naturally induce works in a simpler, more direct style than was customary for concert works of absolute music. But it did not by any means lessen my interest in composing works in an idiom that might be accessible only to cultivated listeners. As I look back, it seems to me that what I was trying for in the simpler works was only partly the writing of compositions that might speak to a broader audience. More than that they gave me an opportunity to try for a more homespun musical idiom, not so different in intention from what attracted me in more hectic fashion in my jazz-influenced works of the twenties. In other words, it was not only musical functionalism that was in question, but also musical language.

This desire of mine to find a musical vernacular, which, as language, would cause no difficulties to my listeners, was perhaps nothing more than a recrudescence of my old interest in making a connection between music and the life about me. Our serious composers have not been signally successful at making that kind of connection. Oblivious to their surroundings, they live in constant communion with great works, which in turn seems to make it *de rigueur* for them to attempt to emulate the great works by writing one of their own on an equivalent plane. Do not misunderstand me. I entirely approve of the big gesture for those who can carry it off. What seems to me a waste of time is the self-deceiving "major" effort on the part of many composers who might better serve the community by the writing of a good piece for high school band. Young composers are especially prone to overreaching themselves — to making the grand gesture by the writing of ambitious works, often in a crabbed style, that have no future whatever. It is unrealistic and a useless aping, generally of foreign models. I have no illusion, of course, that this good advice will be heeded by anyone. But I like to think that in my own work I have, by example, encouraged the notion that a composer writes for different purposes and from different viewpoints. It is a satisfaction to know that in the composing of a ballet like *Billy the Kid* or in a film score like

Our Town, and perhaps in the *Lincoln Portrait,* I have touched off for myself and others a kind of musical naturalness that we have badly needed along with "great" works.

An honest appraisal of the position of the American composer in our society today would find much to be proud of, and also much to complain about. The worst feature of the composer's life is the fact that he does not feel himself an integral part of the musical community. There is no deep need for his activities as composer, no passionate concern in each separate work as it is written. (I speak now not of my own personal experience, but of my observation of the general scene.) When a composer is played he is usually surrounded by an air of mild approval; when he is not played no one demands to hear him. Performances in any case are rare events, with the result that very few composers can hope to earn a livelihood from the music they write. The music-teaching profession has therefore been their principal resource, and the composing of music an activity reserved for their spare time. These are familiar complaints, I know, perhaps immemorial ones; but they show little sign of abatement, and in the aggregate they make composers as a group an unhappy lot, with the outward signs of unhappiness ranging from open resentment to inner frustration.

On the brighter side of the ledger there is the cheering fact that numerically there are many more active composers than there once were. There is private encouragement on the part of certain foundations and individuals, and prizes and commissions are much more frequently given. An occasional radio station or recording company will indicate a spurt of interest. The publishers have shown signs of gratifying awakening, by a willingness to invest in the future of unknowns. The music critics are, generally speaking, more open-minded in their attitude, more ready to applaud than they were a quarter of a century ago. And best of all, there appears to be a continual welling up of new talents from all parts of America that augurs well for our composing future.

In the final analysis the composer must look for keenest satisfaction in the work that he does — in the creative act itself. In many important respects creation in an industrial community is little different from what it has always been in any community. What, after all, do I put down when I put down notes? I put down a reflection of emotional states: feelings, perceptions, imaginings, intuitions. An emotional state, as I use the term, is compounded of everything we are: our background, our environment, our convictions. Art particularizes and makes actual these fluent emotional states. Because it particularizes and because it makes actual, it gives meaning to *la condition humaine*. If it gives meaning it necessarily has purpose. I would even add that it has moral purpose.

One of the primary problems for the composer in an industrial society like that of America is to achieve integration, to find justification for the life of art in the life about him. I must believe in the ultimate good of the world and of life as I live it in order to create a work of art. Negative emotions cannot produce art; positive emotions bespeak an emotion about something. I cannot imagine an art work without implied convictions; and that is true also for music, the most abstract of the arts.

It is this need for a positive philosophy which is a little frightening in the world as we know it. You cannot make art out of fear and suspicion; you can make it only out of affirmative beliefs. This sense of affirmation can be had only in part from one's inner being; for the rest it must be continually reactivated by a creative and yea-saying atmosphere in the life about one. The artist should feel himself affirmed and buoyed up by his community. In other words, art and the life of art must mean something, in the deepest sense, to the everyday citizen. When that happens, America will have achieved a maturity to which every sincere artist will have contributed.

Postscript

THE NORTON PROFESSORSHIP COMMITTEE suggested to me the performance of a certain amount of live music after each of my talks. I readily agreed, for I have often envied the art historian his illustrative slides and the poet his lengthy quotations from the works he admired. In music we have the phonograph; but experience has taught me that one uses the phonograph with only moderate success outside the classroom. The idea of a brief postlecture concert seemed worth trying, although the music chosen for performance had, at times, only indirect relevance to the substance of my lecture. Contact with the live sound of music always helps to dispel that vague and unsatisfactory sensation that follows on any mere discussion of music. These short concerts had the further advantage of forcing me to be as concise as possible, while holding out to my listeners the promise of a dessert to follow on the bare bones of my discourse.

The programs were presented in 1951 on November 13, 20, 27 and in 1952 on March 5, 12, 19. The list here corresponds with the sequence of the six chapters of this book, although in actual presentation the fifth program preceded the fourth.

Programs

1

PATRICIA NEWAY, *Mezzo-soprano*
ARTHUR GOLD, *Pianist*
ROBERT FIZDALE, *Pianist*
JOHN LA MONTAINE, *Accompanist*

CONCERTO PER DUE PIANOFORTI SOLI (1935)   *Igor Stravinsky*
Con Moto; Notturno; Quattro variazioni; Preludio e Fuga

SONGS   *Hector Berlioz*
Absence (1834; revised 1841); La Mort d'Ophélie (1848); La Captive (1832; revised 1834); Au Cimetière (1834; revised 1841); Villanelle (1834; revised 1841)

JEUX D'ENFANTS (1873?) (*Excerpts*)   *Georges Bizet*
La Toupie, Impromptu; Les Quatre Coins, Esquisse; Petit mari, Petite femme, Duo; Le Bal, Galop

SYLVIA MARLOWE, *Harpsichord and Piano*
WOLFE WOLFINSOHN, *Violin*
2 GEORGE FINKEL, *Violoncello*
FRANCES SNOW DRINKER, *Flute*
WILDER E. SCHMALZ, *Oboe*
ROBERT C. STUART, *Clarinet*

SONATA FOR VIOLIN AND HARPSICHORD (1778) K. 301   *Mozart*
Allegro con spirito; Allegro
(*The second movement was repeated with the piano substituted for the harpsichord.*)

LES FASTES DE LA GRANDE ET ANCIENNE MÉNESTRANDISE (pub. 1717)
(*Harpsichord alone*)   *Couperin*
Les Notables et Jurés (marche); Les Vielleux et les Gueux (Bourdon); Les Jongleurs,
Sauteurs et Saltimbanques; Les Invalides; Désordre et déroute de toute la troupe

*CONCERTO PER CLAVICEMBALO, FLAUTO, OBOE, CLARINETTO, VIOLINO
E VIOLONCELLO* (1926)   *de Falla*
Allegro; Lento (giubiloso ed energico); Vivace (flessibile, scherzando)

3 REAH SADOWSKY, *Pianist*
PAUL DES MARAIS, *Pianist*

SONATA IN B FLAT MAJOR (*posthumous*)   *Schubert*
Molto moderato; Andante sostenuto; Scherzo: Allegro vivace; Allegro ma non troppo

PIANO VARIATIONS (1930)   *Copland*

ONDINE (from *GASPARD DE LA NUIT*) (1908)   *Ravel*

NEW MUSIC STRING QUARTET:
BROADUS ERLE, *Violin*
4 MATTHEW RAIMONDI, *Violin*
WALTER TRAMPLER, *Viola*
CLAUS ADAM, *Violoncello*

STRING QUARTET, OPUS 28 (1938)   *Anton Webern*
Mässig; Gemächlich; Sehr fliessend

STRING QUARTET NO. 2 IN F SHARP (1942)   *Michael Tippett*
Allegro grazioso; Andante; Presto; Allegro appassionata

PHYLLIS CURTIN, *Soprano*

5 GEORGE ZAZOFSKY, *Violin*

GREGORY TUCKER, *Piano*

SONATINA FOR VIOLIN AND PIANO (1924)   *Carlos Chavez* (Mexico)

SUITE FOR SOPRANO AND VIOLIN (1923)   *Heitor Villa-Lobos* (Brazil)
A Menina e a Canção; Quéro Ser Alégre; Sertaneja

THREE SONGS   *Alejandro Caturla* (Cuba)
Bito Manué (1931); Dos Poemas Afro-Cubanos (1930): (a) Mari-sabel; (b) Juego santo

THE MUSIC OF LENNIE TRISTANO, DAVE BRUBECK, BUD POWELL, AND OSCAR PETTIFORD (*recorded*)

WILLIAM MASSELOS, *Piano*

6 NEW ENGLAND CONSERVATORY ALUMNI CHORUS,

LORNA COOKE DE VARON, *Conductor*

ELIZABETH DAVIDSON, *Accompanist*

FIRST PIANO SONATA (1902–1909)   *Charles E. Ives*
1. Adagio con moto — andante con moto — allegro risoluto — adagio cantabile; 2. Allegro moderato, "In the Inn": allegro; 3. Largo — allegro — largo, come prima; 4. Allegro — presto (as fast as possible); 5. Andante maestoso — adagio cantabile — allegro — allegro moderato ma con brio

AMERICANA, *chorus of mixed voices* (1932)   *Randall Thompson*
(text from *The American Mercury*)
1. May Every Tongue; 2. The Staff Necromancer; 3. God's Bottles; 5. Loveli — lines

LARK, *mixed chorus with baritone solo* (1938)   *Copland*
(text by Genevieve Taggard)

Sources

For those readers who may wish to know the sources of my principal quotations in the text, I append the following list.

Page   *Introduction*

2   Auden, Wystan H., "Some Reflections on Opera as a Medium," *Partisan Review* (January–February 1952), p. 11.

2–3   Sartre, Jean-Paul, *L'Imaginaire* (Paris: Gallimard, 1940); translation, *The Psychology of Imagination* (New York: The Philosophical Library, 1948), pp. 278–280.

Page	
	Chapter One
7	Coleridge, Samuel T., *Biographia Literaria*, Everyman's Library edition (London: J. M. Dent & Sons, 1949), chapter xiv, p. 153.
10	Bullough, Edward, " 'Psychical Distance' as a Factor in Art and as an Aesthetic Principle," *British Journal of Psychology*, V (1912), part II, pp. 87–118, esp. 91; quoted in Susanne Langer, *Philosophy in a New Key* (Cambridge: Harvard University Press, 1942), pp. 209–210, 223.
10	Claudel, Paul, *The Eye Listens*, translated by Elsie Pell (New York: The Philosophical Library, 1950), p. 209.
12–13	Hanslick, Eduard, *Vom Musikalisch–Schönen* (Leipzig: R. Weigel, 1854), p. 103; quoted in Langer, *Philosophy in a New Key*, p. 238.
13	Langer, Susanne, *Philosophy in a New Key* (Cambridge: Harvard University Press, 1942), chapter viii, pp. 204–245, esp. 245.
13	Santayana, George, *Reason in Art*, vol. IV of *The Life of Reason* (New York, Scribner's Sons, 1905), p. 58.
18–19	Dent, Edward J., "The Historical Approach to Music," *The Musical Quarterly*, XXIII (January 1937), p. 5.
19	Santayana, George, *Three Philosophical Poets* (Cambridge: Harvard University Press, 1910), Introduction, p. 3.

	Chapter Two
26	Wierzynski, Kazimierz, *The Life and Death of Chopin*, translated by N. Guterman, with a Foreword by Artur Rubinstein (New York: Simon and Schuster, 1949), p. 197.
27	Sachs, Curt, *Our Musical Heritage* (New York: Prentice Hall, 1948), pp. 9–28.
31	Schönberg, Arnold, *Style and Idea* (New York: The Philosophical Library, 1950), p. 38.
32	Spender, Stephen, *World Within World* (London: Hamish Hamilton, 1951), p. 93.
39	Chavez, Carlos, *Toward a New Music*, translated by Herbert Weinstock (New York: Norton and Co., 1937), p. 178.

	Chapter Three
41	Maritain, Jacques, *Art and Poetry*, translated by E. deP. Matthews (New York: The Philosophical Library, 1945), p. 89.
42	Coleridge, Samuel T., *Biographia Literaria*, chapter xiv, pp. 151–152. See above.
44	Sessions, Roger, *The Musical Experience of Composer, Performer, Listener* (Princeton: Princeton University Press, 1950), p. 67.
45	Richards, I. A., *Coleridge on Imagination* (New York: Harcourt, Brace & Co., 1935), p. 47.
46	Mellers, Wilfrid, *Music and Society* (New York: Roy Publishers, 1950), p. 206.

	Chapter Four
61	Goldbeck, Frederick, in *Music Today*, Journal of the International Society of Contemporary Music, edited by Rollo H. Myers (London: Denis Dobson, 1949), p. 110.

63   Tovey, Sir Donald F., *Musical Textures*, vol. II of *A Musician Talks* (London: Oxford University Press, 1941), p. 45.

64   Busoni, Ferruccio B., *Sketch of a New Esthetic of Music*, translated from the German by Dr. Th. Baker (New York: G. Schirmer, 1911), p. 5 ff. *See also* Skulsky, Abraham, "Wladimir Vogel," *Musical America*, vol. LXIX, no. 15 (December 1, 1949), p. 7, quoting Busoni.

64   Sessions, Roger, *The Musical Experience of Composer, Performer, Listener*, pp. 62–66. See above.

66   James, William, *As William James Said*, edited by Elizabeth Perkins Aldrich (New York: The Vanguard Press, 1942), p. 109, requoted from James, *The Varieties of Religious Experience* (1902), p. 363.

73   Busoni, Ferruccio B., *Sketch of a New Esthetic of Music*, p. 22. See above.

74   Dent, Edward J., in *Music Today*, p. 102. See above: Goldbeck.

76   Richards, I. A., *Principles of Literary Criticism* (5th ed., New York: Harcourt, Brace & Co., 1934), pp. 25–33.

Chapter Five

86   Mellers, Wilfrid, *Music and Society*, pp. 195–196, quoting Roy Harris. See above.

88   Sargeant, Winthrop, *Jazz: Hot and Hybrid* (New ed., New York: E. P. Dutton & Co., 1946), p. 71.

95   Frank, Waldo, *The Re-discovery of America* (New York: Scribner's Sons, 1929), pp. 56–66 (chapter v, "The Grave of Europe").

95   Howard, John Tasker, "Edward MacDowell," *The International Cyclopedia of Music and Musicians*, edited by Oscar Thompson (5th ed., New York: Dodd, Mead & Co., 1949), p. 1058; quoting from a lecture published in MacDowell, *Critical and Historical Essays* (Boston, 1911).

Chapter Six

107   Barzun, Jacques, "Artist against Society: Some Articles of War," *Partisan Review* (January–February 1952), p. 67.